A Great Place to Work

Creating a Healthy Organizational Climate

Paula Jorde Bloom
Ann Hentschel
Jill Bella

The Director's Toolbox
A Management Series for Early Childhood Administrators

Illustrations – Marc Bermann
Design – Stan Burkat

Library of Congress Cataloging-in-Publication Data

Bloom, Paula Jorde
 A Great Place to Work
 ISBN 978-0-9827082-0-0
 Bloom, Paula J. (Paula Jorde), 1947-
        A great place to work : creating a healthy
    organizational climate / Paula Jorde Bloom, Ann
    Hentschel, Jill Bella.
        p. cm. -- (The director's toolbox : management series
    for early childhood administrators ; 6)
        Includes bibliographical references.
        ISBN-13: 978-0-9827082-0-0
        ISBN-10: 0-9827082-0-3
        1. Early childhood education--United States--
    Administration. 2. Quality of work life.
    3. Educational leadership--United States. 4. Early
    childhood educators--United States.   I. Hentschel,
    Ann, 1961- II. Bella, Jill. III. Title. IV. Series:
    Director's toolbox ; 6.
    LB2822.6.B555 2010   372.12'0973
                                   QBI10-600118

Printed in the United States of America

NEW HORIZONS

Educational Consultants and Learning Resources
P.O. Box 863
Lake Forest, Illinois 60045-0863
(847) 295-8131
(815) 366-7494 FAX
newhorizons4@comcast.net
www.newhorizonsbooks.net

Books in **The Director's Toolbox Management Series** are
available at quantity discounts for use in training programs.
For information on bulk quantity rates or how to purchase a
Trainer's Guide for this book, contact the publisher.

CONTENTS

Chapter

1. **How's the Weather in Your Center?** 1
   - Organizational Climate versus Job Satisfaction...........................3
   - Why Organizational Climate Is So Important 3
   - Ten Dimensions of Organizational Climate 4

2. **Measuring the Climate of Your Program** 21
   - The Benefits of Assessing Work Attitudes 21
   - Components of a Good Survey 23
   - Conducting an Informal Assessment 23
   - Formal Assessment Using the Early Childhood Work
     Environment Survey 25
   - The Work Environment Profile 25
   - What Is the "Best" Climate? 31

3. **Partly Cloudy or Partly Sunny—Viewing the World
   through Different Lenses** 33
   - Directors and Teachers View the World Differently...................34
   - Perception Shapes Our Sense of Reality...............................35
   - Three Perspectives 36
   - Embracing Diversity 38
   - Closing the Gap 41

4. **Changing the Weather—The Director's Role** 43
   - Communicating with Purpose...43
   - Dealing with Conflict 48
   - Cultivating a Culture of Inquiry 51
   - Instilling Norms of Continuous Improvement 53

5. **Ten Ways to Guarantee a Bright Forecast** 55
   - Nurture that Collegial Spirit...55
   - Implement High-Impact Professional Development 58
   - Supervise with a Focus on Reflection and Feedback 61
   - Strive for Clarity in Policies and Procedures 64
   - Explore New Options for Rewards and Recognition 66
   - Expand Teachers' Decision-Making Influence 69
   - Strengthen the Focus on Mission and Vision 72
   - Manage and Protect Time 74
   - Address Adult Needs in the Physical Environment....................77
   - Increase Opportunities for Creativity and Innovation 80

6. Clear Skies Ahead—From Assessment to Action 83

- Maria Increases Teachers' Decision-Making Influence.................83
- Sandra Encourages Greater Collegiality 85
- Carmen Expands Opportunities for Professional Growth 88
- Jon Takes Steps to Improve Supervisory Support 91

7. A Final Word 93

For Further Reading 95

Appendices 99

- A. Early Childhood Work Environment Survey—Short Version 101
- B. Early Childhood Work Environment Survey 103
- C. "I Value a Co-Worker Who Is..." 111
- D. Role Perceptions Questionnaire...113

About the Authors

Paula Jorde Bloom holds a joint appointment as Michael W. Louis Endowed Chair of the McCormick Center for Early Childhood Leadership and professor of early childhood education at National-Louis University in Wheeling, Illinois. As one of the country's leading experts on early childhood leadership and program management issues, Dr. Bloom is a frequent keynote speaker at state, national, and international conferences and consultant to professional organizations and state agencies. Paula received her master's and doctoral degrees from Stanford University.

Ann Hentschel is a training and technical assistance specialist at the McCormick Center for Early Childhood Leadership where she works with a team of assessors conducting on-site quality assessments for the Illinois Quality Counts Quality Rating System. Prior to joining the Center, Ann worked for many years in early care and education both as a classroom teacher and as the director of accredited programs. She received her master's degree in early childhood administration from National-Louis University.

Jill Bella is director of special projects for the McCormick Center, overseeing reliability training for the *Program Administration Scale* (PAS) and quality of work life assessments using the *Early Childhood Work Environment Survey* (ECWES). Jill works with child care resource and referral agencies across the country providing technical assistance on how the PAS and ECWES can be incorporated into director credential and quality enhancement initiatives. Jill received her master's degree from the University of Illinois in child development and early intervention and is currently enrolled in the adult education doctoral program at National-Louis University.

Acknowledgements

First published as a slim turquoise-colored volume by NAEYC in 1988, *A Great Place to Work* sparked the quality of work life movement in the early childhood field. In 1997, some minor revisions were made to the book and NAEYC gave the cover a facelift by changing the color to goldenrod. For over a decade now I've wanted to do a more extensive make-over, incorporating all the great ideas that directors have shared. As with many good intentions, life got in the way and I never quite got around to it. I am so appreciative of the gentle, but forceful, prodding by Ann and Jill. Bless them. They were really the ones who took the initiative to help this revision take flight. Together we have transformed the original book, making it less academic and more consistent with the light-hearted style of the Director's Toolbox Series. We have expanded the content significantly with more concrete strategies for directors to consider, while retaining the book's central thesis that programs can't provide high-quality experiences for children without addressing the human needs of the adults overseeing their care and education.

I am indebted to Carol Copple and the editorial team at NAEYC for their wise guidance over the years. NAEYC has supported so many important initiatives to professionalize the early childhood workforce. Kathy Rousseau helped track down resources for this new edition and Heather Knapp provided data from the *Early Childhood Work Environment Survey*. As with the other volumes in the Director's Toolbox Series, Catherine Cauman has done a great job of editing the manuscript. And finally, special thanks to my wonderful colleagues at the McCormick Center for Early Childhood Leadership who show me every day the amazing power of a great place to work.

PJB

CHAPTER 1

How's the Weather in Your Center?

If you've visited many other early childhood programs, you know that each has its own distinct personality. Some seem to exude warmth and sunlight from the moment you walk in the door. The director and teachers are spirited and energetic. They radiate a sense of confidence and enthusiasm about their work. When they interact with children, families, and each other, they are warmhearted and supportive. In other settings, though, stormy conditions seem to permeate the air. The mood may be competitive or harsh. Spontaneous laughter is infrequent and complaints about roles and responsibilities, general work conditions, and, of course, *those* parents, are frequent.

Each program's personality and characteristics certainly affect the quality of work life for staff. Organizational theorists refer to the distinct atmosphere that characterizes work settings as its *organizational climate*. The use of a weather metaphor seems appropriate because some centers are distinctly sunny, warm, and nurturing, while others are stormy and unpredictable.

Most of us do not stop to analyze the organizational climate of our workplace, but the climate does influence our behavior, our feelings about our jobs, and how comfortable we feel in expressing our opinions. Without question, the climate of our programs impacts how well we perform our responsibilities and the quality of our day-to-day interactions with children, parents, and co-workers.

Although organizational climate may be relatively easy to sense even in a brief visit, the concept is not easy to define. It is made up of many dimensions, including the perceptions, attitudes, beliefs, and values of all the individuals in a work setting—a composite of personalities and the leadership that guides them. Your role as director and the decisions you make as a leader have a big impact on staff's perceptions of the organizational climate of your program.

If you work in an early care and education setting, take a moment to assess the current weather conditions at your center by completing Exercise 1 on the following page.

Using weather terminology, how would you describe your center?

Clear Skies

Lightening

Light Showers

Arctic Blast

Sunny

Bitter Cold

Gentle Breeze

Windy

Blistering Hot

Thick Fog

Partly Cloudy

Storm Brewing

Calm and Tranquil

Strong Headwinds

Muggy

Tornado

Tsunami

Frosty

Hurricane-Force Winds

Hazy

Downpour

High Pressure

Overcast

The weather at my center is: _____

_____

_____

Organizational Climate versus Job Satisfaction

Organizational climate is not the same as *psychological climate* or *job satisfaction*, which are people's perceptions of the degree to which their own individual needs and expectations are being met. Organizational climate, on the other hand, describes workers' collective perceptions of conditions that exist in the workplace.

Organizational climate and job satisfaction are closely related. Although it is not clear whether climate or satisfaction comes first, job satisfaction seems higher in programs with relatively open, healthy climates. Healthy climates are characterized by a sense of belonging, warm and caring interactions, a collective sense of purpose, and upward influence.

Whenever people work together, they individually and jointly affect each other and their environment. Job descriptions may define different jobs, but individuals shape their roles according to their skills and attitudes. Each person influences the collective values and work orientation of the group. At the same time, people's attitudes and behavior are shaped by the environment in which they work.

This pattern of relationships has been called a *social ecological* model of human behavior because it stresses the dynamic, interactive nature between people and their environment. The model fits well with the concept of organizational climate because the collective perceptions of workers are influenced by differences in organizational structure as well as by individual meanings that people attach to their interactions.

Why Organizational Climate Is So Important

Some theorists define organizational climate as a *global perception* of the quality of an organization. This does not mean, however, that climate is unidimensional. Many different organizational practices contribute to the global perception people have about their work environment.

It is important to remember that these perceptions are *subjective interpretations* that vary between people and may not reflect reality. Individuals perceive the meaning of events differently, depending on their role in an organization, their value orientation, and the context of the situation. For example, directors consistently view organizational practices more favorably than do the teachers. We'll look at this phenomenon in greater detail in Chapter 3.

Taking steps to improve your center's organizational climate is an effective way to increase staff morale, enhance program quality, and perhaps even reduce teacher turnover. Several studies have found a significant relationship between staff commitment and organizational climate. In a field plagued with high turnover, it makes good sense to direct our attention toward establishing work environments that foster high levels of commitment.

One important characteristic of a healthy climate that inspires commitment is a warm, caring relationship among administrators, teachers, and support staff. Your program may be a business, but it is a people business. As such the relationships established among your staff are at the core of the success of the program. As the distinguished scholar Roland Barth states, "Teachers and administrators demonstrate all too well a capacity to either enrich or diminish one another's lives and thereby enrich or diminish their program."

We've all experienced working in good and bad groups. Have you ever wondered what factors cause some groups to jell and others to disintegrate? Groups that are cohesive are often described with phrases such as "Everything just clicked," "We felt instant rapport," or "It was fate," while bad groups are characterized with phrases that place the blame on people, such as "poor leadership," "bad chemistry," or "personality defects."

It is interesting that leadership is often overlooked when describing the success of good groups. This is odd, since research tells us that successful, thriving organizations depend heavily on capable leadership. If you are looking for a surefire formula to create a work environment that generates a dynamic, committed, and capable team, a good starting point is to consider the dimensions of organizational climate and how they apply to your program.

Ten Dimensions of Organizational Climate

To better understand the dimensions of organizational climate, we must take into account the research on school effectiveness, group dynamics, work attitudes, and the interplay between people and their environments. The ten dimensions described in the following table arise from a practical sense about how early childhood centers differ, and are consistent with present theoretical knowledge about individual and group behavior in organizations. There is certainly some overlap between these ten dimensions, as the categories are not meant to be mutually exclusive.

Ten Dimensions of Organizational Climate

Dimension	Definition
Collegiality	The extent to which staff are friendly, supportive, and trusting of one another. The peer cohesion and esprit de corps of the group.
Professional Growth	The degree of emphasis placed on staff's professional growth. The availability of opportunities to increase professional competence.
Supervisor Support	The degree of facilitative leadership providing encouragement, support, and clear expectations.
Clarity	The extent to which policies, procedures, and responsibilities are clearly defined and communicated.
Reward System	The degree of fairness and equity in the distribution of pay, fringe benefits, and opportunities for advancement.
Decision Making	The degree of autonomy given to staff and the extent to which they are involved in making centerwide decisions.
Goal Consensus	The extent to which staff agree on the philosophy, goals, and educational objectives of the center.
Task Orientation	The emphasis placed on organizational effectiveness and efficiency, including productive meetings, program outcomes, and accountability.
Physical Setting	The extent to which the spatial arrangement of the center helps or hinders staff in carrying out their responsibilities. The availability of supplies and materials.
Innovativeness	The extent to which the center adapts to change and encourages staff to find creative ways to solve problems.

From Bloom, P. J. (2010). *Measuring work attitudes in the early childhood setting.* Wheeling, IL: McCormick Center for Early Childhood Leadership, National-Louis University. Reprinted with permission.

Collegiality. People are social. All of us need to feel that others care about us and are concerned about our welfare. You already know from your own experience in different work settings that emotional support can be a potent force in creating a positive work climate. When staff genuinely care and trust one another, an esprit de corps develops. The rationale for providing an environment that fosters friendly, supportive relationships is well grounded in research about job satisfaction and personal self-fulfillment.

There is compelling evidence in the research literature that collegiality is characteristic of high-achieving elementary schools. In effective schools, teachers value and participate in a wide range of professional interactions with one another—they plan together, talk about pedagogy together, and engage in structured observations of each other's classrooms.

Schools with a strong sense of collegiality are characterized by a unified team spirit, a collective sense of efficacy, and the absence of social cliques. Teachers are loyal to the school, and sharing information and resources with one another is the norm. Interactions are comfortable and individuals feel free to express their thoughts openly. These schools give high priority to minimizing teacher isolation.

These same patterns of collegiality characterize effective early care and education programs. In all these settings, though, the appropriate degree of collegiality varies depending on the formal and informal structures of the program and the needs and expectations of staff members. Take a moment to think about the collegial interactions at your center as you complete Exercise 2.

Exercise 2

Select three words from the possibilities below that most accurately describe relations among the staff at your center:

cooperative	friendly	isolated	cautious
competitive	trusting	guarded	helpful
caring	cliquish	open	mistrustful

As you reflect on the nature of co-worker relations at your center, here are a few questions to ask yourself:

- How do teachers show their commitment to the center? Do they speak positively about the program? Are they willing to put in extra effort above and beyond their required job responsibilities?

- How do teachers approach group projects? Is there a sense of teamwork and shared responsibility, or do the same teachers always seem to volunteer and shoulder the workload?

- How comfortable are teachers about sharing their opinions and feelings on different issues? Do they openly offer their ideas and thoughts on different topics, or do they need to be coaxed to open up and express their point of view? Are they willing to discuss contentious issues in a calm and rationale way?

Professional growth. In some centers, teachers are unaware of what others in the early childhood field are doing in their classrooms and rarely share ideas and resources. In contrast, centers that value professional development find creative ways to pay staff expenses for conferences and workshops, provide release time to visit other programs, reimburse tuition for college courses, and stock a library with a variety of professional magazines, journals, training DVDs, and curriculum guides.

The degree of emphasis on opportunities for professional growth is closely related to management priorities. Schools that have a strong professional orientation maximize opportunities for teachers to reflect on and evaluate their instructional practices. These programs plan opportunities for teachers to expand their knowlege base and widen their repertoire of competencies. At the same time, they create a nonthreatening atmosphere in which teachers are encouraged to help one another.

In her research on effective schools, Judith Warren Little has found that when professional development is a high priority, teachers engage in frequent, continuous, and precise talk about teaching practices. They plan, design, research, prepare, and evaluate teaching materials together. But more importantly, they are encouraged to regularly reflect on their performance, evaluate feedback, and examine new and alternative practices.

High-growth climates tailor in-service staff development activities to individuals' differing needs, and they tie opportunities for professional advancement to a well-defined career ladder. Programs with these climates encourage teachers to stretch and develop their potential. This is particularly important in times when there is increasing emphasis on accountability and standards-based education for children.

The landscape of our field has changed significantly with the nationwide adoption of early learning standards. In a joint position statement, the National Association of Early Childhood Specialists in State Departments of Education (NAECS/SDE) and the National Association for the Education of Young Children (NAEYC) stress the importance of professional development:

> *Significant expansion of professional development is essential if all early childhood teachers and administrators are to gain the knowledge, skills, and dispositions needed to implement early learning standards. Well-educated, knowledgeable, and caring teachers are the key to positive outcomes for children. Efforts to create early learning standards must be accompanied by in-depth professional development, coaching, and mentoring for teachers, administrators, and teacher educators—not just about the standards themselves, but also about the appropriate curriculum, teaching strategies, relationships, and assessment tools that together make up a systematic approach to improving outcomes for all children.*

Although staff development is usually advocated as a way to improve teachers' skill in working with children, it should also be recognized as an important ingredient in a satisfying and stimulating professional life. Staff development experiences that are designed to solve practical problems and meet the personal needs of teachers can make an important contribution to both the quality of teaching and the satisfaction that teachers feel in their professional lives.

Take a tour through your center with the perspective of a new staff member. What things do you see that provide evidence of the ongoing professional development of the staff? When you are done, take a few minutes to complete Excerise 3.

Indicate all the items in this professional development checklist that describe current practices at your center.

☐ The center has a professional resource library accessible to all staff.

☐ Supervisors meet regularly with individual staff members to support their professional growth.

☐ Mentors are assigned to new teachers to help orient them to the program.

☐ Teachers attend more in-service training hours than required by state licensing.

☐ Professional development opportunities are posted on a staff bulletin board, distributed in teachers' mailboxes, and promoted at staff meetings.

☐ The program pays for teachers' membership for at least one professional organization.

☐ The program provides compensation for staff to attend workshops and conferences held off-site.

☐ The program provides tuition reimbursement for college classes.

☐ Teachers are given release time to observe one another's classrooms and visit other centers.

☐ Teachers are encouraged to share information at staff meetings about professional development experiences they've attended.

☐ Teaching and administrative staff are encouraged to present workshops at local and regional conferences.

☐ Some time is devoted at every staff meeting for professional development (e.g., a discussion about an article that everyone has read).

☐ Professional achievements of team members are highlighted on the center's bulletin boards, in newsletters, at meetings, or on the center's website.

☐ There is a career ladder for advancement that encourages increases in experience, specialized training, and general education.

☐ The center subscribes to educational journals and magazines and makes them available to staff.

Supervisor support. One of the most important ingredients supporting high-quality early childhood programming is consistent and facilitative supervision that provides clear expectations and encouragement. All teachers need to know they are valued for their hard work. A supervisor's psychological support may well have a more enduring impact on a teacher's self-esteem and overall performance than any tangible resources that are provided. In studies of different industries, including education, about one-fourth of employees cite a lack of appreciation by their supervisor as their reason for leaving their jobs.

Still, teachers need more than just recognition or an appreciative pat on the back. A supportive supervisor gives open, honest, and regular feedback that is respectful of the individual's feelings of self-worth and provides direction for personal and professional improvement. The link is well established—focused feedback helps broaden teachers' repertoire of instructional strategies and increases classroom effectiveness.

Research on supervisor-employee relations has consistently found that supervisors underestimate how powerful their feedback to their employees is in motivating high performance. Unfortunately, many early childhood programs are so tightly staffed that new teachers are often turned loose in the classroom with only a brief orientation to the program. Feedback, if given at all, is reserved for the dreaded once-a-year performance appraisal conference.

We are working in an era in which education standards require more formalized requirements for teacher accountability. This creates a certain tension in your role as supervisor. You are expected to impose certain standardized criteria on teachers' performance while at the same time encouraging autonomy and respect for an individual's professional judgment. Certainly, all teachers deserve and desire a degree of autonomy in designing quality experiences for children; however, leaving teachers completely on their own to handle the wide range of daily challenges they face in their classrooms contributes to feelings of isolation. Professional judgment and autonomy can still exist in a supportive environment.

The types of support you offer as a supervisor should vary according to the developmental stage of each teacher. Teachers who are inexperienced and less knowledgeable benefit from direct feedback, intervention, and concrete support. Teachers who are more experienced, competent, and self-assured benefit from a more nondirective approach to providing feedback that involves listening, asking open-ended questions, and encouraging self-reflection.

So ask yourself: Do I have the pulse of what is going on in each classroom and the particular challenges the teachers face? Do the teachers seek my opinion when problems occur in their classrooms? Does my supervisory style cultivate a

People will forget what you said, people will forget what you did, but people will never forget how you made them feel.

Maya Angelou

culture of helpfulness? Early childhood programs with well-defined systems of teacher support are organized for steady improvement, and they build and nurture professional competence through clear, direct, and unambiguous supervisor feedback that focuses on behavior and action. Directors in these centers are truly instructional leaders guiding staff performance.

Clarity. Every early childhood program operates with a complex network of roles, relationships, and expectations, so the way policies, procedures, and responsibilities are defined and carried out deeply influence the program's effectiveness. Only when roles and responsibilities are clearly defined can employees understand how their jobs mesh with the expectations of others.

Lack of clear job descriptions can create conflict among staff. If policies or procedures are vague, problems arise when people try to communicate. Poorly defined rules and regulations can result in confusion and add to job stress. In contrast, order and clarity are positively related to job satisfaction and higher levels of performance. Thus, effective management practices in this area have a direct impact on reducing role-related stress.

So, why is clarity so important in early care and education? In early childhood programs, teacher assistants, teachers, and lead teachers may all have similar duties, ranging from maintenance work to planning curriculum and conducting parent conferences. Tension often results when job title and pay do not distinguish between who does what, why, and when. In our field, distinctions in responsibilities based on job title are related more to the amount of time spent performing tasks than to the nature of the tasks themselves.

The results of several studies about the early childhood workforce reveal that the lack of clarity in programs is a serious issue. A study of centers across the country using the *Program Administration Scale*, for example, found that more than one-half of programs do not have performance appraisals linked by role to specific job responsibilities. While two thirds of programs have a written salary scale, less than one-half of programs make this information available to all center staff. In many centers, teachers even work without a written contract. Another study found that the frequency of communication at a center (e.g., the number of staff meetings held) was related to employees' positive or negative work attitudes.

Communication in programs with a healthy organizational climate is consistent, clear, and unambiguous. There is agreement among staff about who is to do what, how, and when. Information is direct and open, and it flows both vertically (to and from administrators and staff) and horizontally (among employees in similar positions). No doubt about it, many of the problems experienced in programs could be prevented by having clear policies and procedures.

So ask yourself, how clear are the policies and procedures at your center? Here are questions to consider:

- Are there any policies that staff aren't currently following?

- Is anything happening at the center that shows a need to clarify an existing policy?

- Have teachers been doing things in incorrect or inefficient ways that could be improved with clearer procedures?

- Are there conflicting expectations about who is responsible for certain tasks?

- Could job descriptions reflect responsibilities better?

- Do policies in the employee handbook sometimes contradict policies stated elsewhere?

Of course, clarity is not something that can be achieved and then forgotten. Roles, responsibilities, and regulations must be updated regularly to meet the changing needs of a healthy workplace.

Reward system. Your own experience probably confirms the prevailing view that early childhood teachers enter the field for reasons other than salary, benefits, job security, promotion opportunities, and professional prestige. You are also probably sadly aware that teachers often leave their jobs for these very reasons. A number of studies have consistently found that most early childhood workers feel underpaid and undervalued by society. Particularly in tough economic times, teachers are often forced to leave the jobs they love to find ones that provide better remuneration and security.

Professional and advocacy organizations such as the NAEYC and the Center for the Child Care Workforce (CCW) consider compensation and working conditions priority issues. Our society obviously must resolve some deep and complicated problems about the funding of early childhood programs. Both prospective and practicing teachers are influenced by salary levels. The number of teachers who leave for other occupations is directly related to salary, as is the number of new entrants into the field.

Even as we wrestle with these issues on a national basis, directors can take steps to ensure that their staff feel confident that their center's compensation practices are fair and just. Healthy organizational climates include a reward system with fair and equitably administered pay, job security, and promotion policies. A means to ensure such a reward system is to consider both internal and external equity. The accompanying table summarizes the key aspects of internal and external equity.

Internal Equity

Internal equity refers to the relationships of different jobs within the center. Internal equity has two aspects: the relative similarities and differences in work content of jobs, and the relative value or contribution of the work to the center's goals. Internal equity is achieved through job analysis, the development of job descriptions, and the evaluation of jobs to determine a structure based upon the value of various job's contributions to the organization's goals. There are two types of internal equity.

- **Equal pay for equal work.** Equal (or substantially similar) work means work requiring similar behaviors and tasks being performed under similar working conditions, and work requiring similar responsibilities, efforts, and abilities (e.g., a preschool teacher and an infant/toddler teacher).

- **Equal pay for comparable worth.** The yardstick for achieving this aspect of internal equity is determining the relative worth of different jobs in the center as they contribute to the overall mission of the center (e.g., a preschool teacher and the administrative assistant).

External Equity

External equity refers to the relationship of jobs among employers in the external labor market. External equity is established by determining the going rate for similar work in relevant labor markets. There are two types of external equity.

- **Equal pay for equal work.** How do other centers pay for equal or substantially similar work? To apply this standard, it is necessary to determine the relevant comparison group and whether the work content of the different jobs is really equal. The guiding principle is that early childhood professionals with comparable qualifications, experience, and job responsibilities should receive comparable compensation, regardless of the setting of their job. Thus, a teacher in a nonprofit, community child care center, a family child care provider, and a prekindergarten teacher at a public school who have comparable qualifications should receive comparable compensation.

- **Equal pay for comparable worth.** This area of external equity is the most difficult to assess. We know for a variety of reasons (market forces and the devaluation of "women's work") that early childhood workers earn less than half as much as comparably educated women and less than one-third as much as comparably educated men in the civilian labor force. For the present, however, statutory provisions have not provided an easy remedy for evaluating the relative worth of dissimilar jobs and reducing inequities across occupations.

Although the importance of pay as a source of motivation is often downplayed in teacher reports of job satisfaction, the extrinsic rewards workers receive are important for their symbolic value. Pay correlates with esteem—the value society places on teaching. Money means different things to different people. For some, it is a powerful motivator that represents status and security. For others, it is a legitimate form of recognition. Money also has symbolic value because it is an important indicator of equity.

Teachers compare wages, both within and outside their program. For many workers, questions of equity may be just as important as questions of adequacy. Some workers may even unconsciously or consciously match their efforts to their perceptions about their pay.

Promotion also has strong symbolic importance. Many teachers regard it as recognition of high performance. For others, opportunities for advancement offer a sense of future security. For some, especially those in the early stages of their careers, the likelihood of promotion may be more important than current wages.

The mandate is clear. Even if the prevailing headwinds make additional funding for early childhood unlikely, directors need to take steps to ensure internal equity in their programs. They must look for creative ways to reward and recognize their program's most valuable resource, the teachers.

Decision making. What kinds of decisions are made at your center and who makes them? The decision-making structure of an early childhood program determines how power is distributed and how much influence the teaching and administrative staff have in making decisions that impact program functioning.

In general, when teachers feel that their program's decision-making structure is fair and values their input, they are more likely to make a commitment to program goals. Centers with positive organizational climates encourage staff to take an active role in centerwide decision making. Research suggests that staff participation in making decisions also has a positive impact on the level of job satisfaction they experience.

As we'll see in Chapter 3, some discrepancies in perception are typical in the dimension of decision making. Administrators and teachers do not always agree on how decision-making influence is distributed; and from the employees' perspective, the actual and the desired amount of influence may differ. Most teachers desire more involvement in decision making, especially regarding issues that directly affect their performance in the classroom.

Determining the appropriate level of participation in decision making depends on the nature of the issue and the people involved. Another book in the Director's Toolbox Management Series, *Circle of Influence: Implementing Shared Decision*

Making and Participative Management, provides detailed guidance on how to structure greater involvement that is genuine and helpful.

Certainly it is not easy to involve staff and keep them informed. If you are serious about including teachers in centerwide decision making, begin by reviewing the range of decisions that are made in your early childhood program. The following table provides examples of decisions in different categories. The list is by no means exhaustive, but it does give a representative sample of the many kinds of decisions that you and your staff make on a regular basis. Use this list as a template for thinking about which kinds of decisions benefit from input and for determining the level of teacher participation.

Types of Decisions

Staff supervision and professional development
- establish guidelines and procedures for staff orientation
- determine the type and frequency of in-service training
- determine professional development plans for staff

Instructional practices and scheduling
- determine the daily schedule of classroom activities
- select instructional materials and equipment
- determine the content and timeline of the curriculum

Enrollment and grouping
- determine group size and patterns (e.g., mixed-age grouping)
- determine grouping assignments
- determine the placement of children with special needs

Fiscal policies and practices
- set priorities for center and classroom expenditures
- determine fundraising priorities and goals

Human resources allocation
- determine the staffing pattern and teaching assignments
- set staff work schedules
- determine the criteria for promotion and advancement

Centerwide goals and educational objectives
- determine the center's philosophy
- determine the educational objectives for different age groups
- determine staff meeting agendas

Parent relations
- determine who serves as primary contact with parents
- determine the type and frequency of parent education
- determine the content of the parent newsletter

Community relations
- determine the type of contacts with community agencies
- establish marketing and public relations priorities
- determine the type of contact with local schools

Facilities management
- determine how space is allocated
- determine how space is arranged
- determine capital improvement priorities

Evaluation practices (child, staff, center)
- determine the type and frequency of child assessments
- determine guidelines for staff performance appraisals
- determine the type and frequency of programwide evaluations

Goal consensus. Educational goals establish priorities—what we want children to do, to be, or to have as a result of their early childhood experience. Employees need to have a common vision for the program so their efforts can be consistently directed toward goals. The flip side of goal consensus is conflict and divisiveness.

Take a look at the following six educational objectives that are typical in early care and education programs in this country:

- to help children develop language and problem-solving skills

- to help children build strong friendships and learn to share

- to help children master concepts needed for reading and arithmetic

- to help children develop skill and independence in caring for themselves

- to help children develop physical coordination

- to help children develop healthy self-esteem and a positive self-concept

Make a mental note of the educational objective you feel is most important for your program, your top priority. Now look at the remaining educational objectives and consider which one you believe is the second most important. How about the least important? The fact is, all these educational objectives are noble—every single one is worthy of our attention. However, the reality is that programs need to establish priorities for how time is spent and how resources are allocated. We simply can't pursue all these educational objectives with the same degree of zeal. How confident are you that your teachers would select the same educational objectives as their most, second most, and least important priorities?

As you've probably experienced, achieving goal consensus is not easy. Differences in philosophy, socioeconomic status, background, experiences, and tradition are bound to contribute to differences in value orientation. Goal consensus thus reflects the ability of staff to compromise and tolerate differences of opinion so that individuals can work toward a common vision.

Previous research provides some clues as to how goal consensus may impact the quality of teaching practices and overall program effectiveness in educational settings. In elementary schools, for example, research shows that ambiguous goals and a lack of unifying purpose lead to greater instructional uncertainty. In such schools, teachers tend to define and independently pursue their own goals. This reinforces norms of self-reliance rather than collaboration. The result is reduced professional interaction and feelings of isolation.

In early childhood settings where turnover is high, it is particularly difficult to achieve a unified goal orientation. Directors can take steps, though, to ensure that conversations about values, beliefs, and educational priorities are woven into daily discussions. More importantly, they can involve teachers in a regular review of the center's mission and purpose. Through involvement in goal setting and strategic planning, teachers are more likely to achieve buy-in, feel empowered, and become more committed to the organization.

A goal without a plan is just a wish.

Antoine de Saint Éxupéry

Task orientation. Good planning, efficiency, and getting the job done are the essence of task orientation. In early childhood programs with a healthy organizational climate, time is used wisely and teachers are not burdened with unnecessary busywork. Meetings are well planned and purposeful, and procrastination is an exception rather than the rule.

In your program, are deadlines met? Do meetings start on time? Is there a sense of momentum and progress in projects undertaken? Programs that have a good task orientation tend to be efficient, with an eye on achieving outcomes.

But it is also possible for work environments to be obsessed with efficiency. Workplaces like this are too rigid and controlling and create a stifling work atmosphere. When this kind of "punch-clock" mentality exists, teachers are expected to adhere to strict schedules and time is viewed as a scarce resource. Such an atmosphere can foreclose opportunities for spontaneous activity and decrease staff empowerment.

A healthy work climate balances efficiency and organization with flexibility. Just as teachers and parents expect children to work to their potential, staff perform at their best when a program operates efficiently, personnel are used effectively, and activities are coordinated so people are neither overloaded nor idle. In a healthy organization, everyone works hard, but there is a good fit between people's dispositions and program demands.

Physical setting. The spatial arrangement of the workplace can play a powerful role in shaping attitudes about work and influencing moods, dispositions, and employee morale. Although research in business and industry shows that favorable attitudes about buildings, facilities, materials, and equipment seldom produce the type of job satisfaction that improves work performance, this may not be the case in early care and education.

Why? Because the spatial arrangement of a center strongly influences children's behavior and thus a teacher's ability to carry out the program's educational objectives. Temperature, light, color, noise, ventilation, design, and the layout of furniture can help or hinder staff. Poorly equipped environments or those that have insufficient space are frustrating and stressful places in which to work.

Early childhood programs that have a healthy organizational climate with regard to the physical setting give particular attention to the spatial arrangement and design of the classroom and support space. Support space includes such areas as the lobby and reception foyer, hallways, staff lounge, kitchen, storage areas, and multipurpose common areas. When space is well organized, aesthetically pleasing, and furnished with the proper equipment, materials, and resources, staff can carry out their work more efficiently and effectively.

Interestingly, the physical setting can also reflect the overall climate of a center. When people work in a place they perceive to be negative and unsatisfying, they tend not to want to take care of the environment. The building may appear run down, drab, or "institutional." Thus, physical appearance may well be an indicator of the general organizational health of the program.

Take a few moments to think critically about the physical environment of your center. Are there walls that need to be painted, screens that need to be repaired, equipment that needs to be replaced? What message does the physical appearance of your center convey to staff, children, families, and visitors?

Innovativeness. Early childhood centers, like all organizations, must adapt to change in order to survive. An innovative atmosphere encourages people to find creative ways to solve problems. Diversity is valued in these settings, so new educational approaches and techniques are welcomed. In contrast, programs stuck in the status quo are kind of like those hot, muggy, humid days in August when the air is heavy and breathing is difficult. Such centers are often characterized by complacency, conformity, and a rigid adherence to tradition. In subtle ways they discourage people from offering ideas and providing suggestions to improve program practices.

A spirit of innovation and vibrancy in programs doesn't just happen. It has to be cultivated. Early childhood administrators can initiate or inhibit change. They can build or erode innovativeness in their staff, and they can encourage or stifle experimentation.

Research conducted at the elementary and secondary levels has found that a program's innovativeness primarily depends on a leadership style that encourages receptivity to new ideas and not on the size of the school's financial resources. In examining differences between effective and less effective high schools, for example, Sara Lawrence Lightfoot found that what distinguished exemplary schools was their "consciousness of imperfection"—their willingness to look at their imperfections and create a climate of continual improvement.

Research at the early childhood level, as well, reveals the degree of innovativeness of a program is directly linked to the leadership style of its director. Directors are typically the ones who sense the need for change, set the pace for the change process, and then monitor progress as new ideas are translated into action. Innovative directors are responsive to the concerns of teachers, parents, and the community. They empower people to analyze problems and plan corrective action. They then provide staff with the time, space, and money so ideas can be put into practice.

Creativity is the ability to give the world something it didn't know it was missing.

Daniel Pink

19

We've covered a lot in this first chapter. We hope we've convinced you that tuning in to the factors that impact the organizational climate of your center is not a luxury. It is the essence of what it means to be an effective leader guiding and shaping the quality of work life for those who give so much to others. The ten dimensions of organizational climate are critical in every early childhood work environment. Now that you've looked at some of the factors that determine whether work environments are personally and professionally satisfying, you can begin to assess how well your own program measures in these dimensions.

CHAPTER 2

Measuring the Climate of Your Program

For decades the leaders of business and industry have invested big bucks in evaluating the organizational climate of their different enterprises. Even in educational settings at the elementary and secondary level, many principals regularly engage in climate assessment. Little attention has been focused, however, on the unique aspects of early childhood work settings as they relate to organizational climate. Early childhood programs are strikingly different from other work environments in areas such as funding structure, decision-making hierarchy, supervisory methods, professional roles, and the nature of the work itself. Consequently, most of the instruments designed for other work settings are not practical for assessing the quality of our unique professional work climate.

This chapter provides an overview of the importance of assessing work attitudes. It looks at the benefits of informal and formal assessment and describes in detail one organizational climate tool, the *Early Childhood Work Environment Survey*, intended for use specifically in center-based programs serving young children. You'll be introduced to both the long version and the short version of this instrument. These formal and informal tools will bring to life how the ten dimensions of organizational climate outlined in Chapter 1 can be used to evaluate your program's effectiveness. This chapter describes only the assessment process, though. Hold tight, we'll get to specific strategies you can use to apply the survey results later on, in Chapter 5.

The Benefits of Assessing Work Attitudes

As director, you probably have an overall impression of when things are going well or not so well, but you may lack specific information on just which areas of the program contribute to those impressions. The information gleaned from assessing work attitudes will help you clarify those vague feelings and define more precisely how different dimensions of your center are perceived.

Your staff's perceptions of the center's work climate are a good source of information not necessarily because they reflect objective reality, but rather because how staff perceive their experience is what is important. A systematic method to measure staff perceptions of organizational climate can be useful to:

- clarify feelings about work

- gauge personal and organizational efficiency and effectiveness

- help explain why and where things are going well

- identify where changes are needed

- promote better problem solving

- increase staff involvement

- give direction to program priorities

- target areas for staff development

- improve overall morale and performance

- help ensure that the center stays vibrant

To solve problems and handle conflicts more effectively, directors must establish a climate that invites feedback and supports open discussion of differences. When issues are not dealt with openly, teachers can feel manipulated. Such feelings can affect their commitment to your program.

One valuable insight gained during an assessment of employee attitudes about their work environment is a sharper understanding of where perceptions differ between administrators and employees. One of the more common findings, for example, is that directors often believe they give far more feedback to their teachers than the teachers think they get. Another common difference is in directors' and teachers' perceptions regarding staff involvement in decisions about different organizational policies and practices.

The objectives, content, and emphasis of in-service programs for staff development can all be shaped by analyzing the work climate. The assessment process also helps you answer important questions that will aid in establishing your center's priorities. Which issues are most pressing? How can the center's resources be used to the best advantage? Where is additional support needed?

Even if you are not aware of any immediate problems, a periodic survey of work attitudes is helpful. One way to ensure that your center stays vibrant is to regularly monitor employee perceptions of different organizational practices.

School climate is much like the air we breathe—it tends to go unnoticed until something is seriously wrong.

H. Jerome Freiberg

22

When used in this way, the assessment can be a preventive measure by directing energy away from griping and toward finding solutions before issues develop into problems. Two-way communication between you and your staff can increase simply because everyone is engaged in the common task of improving the work environment.

Components of a Good Survey

When assessing work attitudes, it is tempting to just jump in, create a quick survey, and distribute it to everyone. To produce beneficial results, though, an attitude survey must meet three requirements.

Surveys should have a clear purpose. The purpose of the survey should be stated clearly and understood by all concerned, including the board of directors and others involved in the operation of your program. The process should convey to your employees that feedback is important in improving the efficiency and effectiveness of the center. It should be clearly stated that the results will not be used to embarrass people or to undermine individuals who have problems; surveys are intended for constructive purposes. This helps prevent apprehension and defensiveness and assure wholehearted participation.

Responses should be confidential. Accurate information can be obtained only if respondents are certain that their answers will be anonymous. Therefore, any questionnaire about work attitudes should be scored by a neutral person who will maintain confidentiality about the results. Otherwise, the information may be inaccurate and of limited value.

Information about results should be shared. Results (favorable or unfavorable) must be shared with the entire group. By doing so, you communicate your concern for the staff's welfare and your intent to be open and to support needed changes. This step can in itself contribute to healthier staff relations by opening channels of communication and stimulating group problem solving. When the results are translated into follow-up activities, teachers will feel a greater sense of professional investment and shared responsibility in implementing change and incorporating new practices.

Conducting an Informal Assessment

Designing your own survey allows you to tailor questions to address specific elements of your program and even target staff who work with a particular age group (infant-toddler teachers, preschool teachers), who hold different roles (assistants, teachers, support staff, and administrators), or who have different work schedules (full-time, part-time, and volunteer workers).

If you are interested in developing your own informal survey, definitely incorporate your staff's ideas when you design your questionnaire. Together, you and the staff can select key questions about your program that tap into each of the dimensions discussed in Chapter 1.

Items can be worded either in a forced-response format (yes/no, multiple choice, or ranking on a scale) or as open-ended questions. Forced-response questions are easier to score and help ensure consistency in interpretation, but sometimes the answers do not accurately reflect the individual's opinion. Open-ended questions take more time to score and make it more likely that the individual can be identified, but they may elicit more specific comments.

Directors have used a variety of approaches to collect information about how their employees perceive their professional work climate. Regardless of your approach, you will probably want to administer an organizational climate assessment at least once a year, and preferably at the same time each year.

You can initiate the process by describing the assessment activity at a staff meeting or distributing a memo to staff members. Either way, comment briefly on why organizational assessment benefits everyone, how confidentiality will be maintained, what will happen with the information collected, and why it is important for everyone to participate. Staff also need to be told about the logistics of when and where to complete the survey.

You may want to distribute the surveys at a staff meeting. If you do, make sure everyone has enough time to complete the surveys and sufficient privacy to keep responses confidential. Each person should receive a plain envelope in which to return the questionnaire.

If you give out a survey at the end of the day, ask that staff members not discuss their responses with one another and request that all surveys be returned in a plain envelope to a designated location. Be sure to give staff a deadline for returning the surveys; usually one to two days works well. Unless at least 80% of the staff returns their surveys, the results will not be very helpful to you.

Appendix A is an example of an informal organizational assessment. This is the short version of the *Early Childhood Work Environment Survey* (ECWES). Feel free to reproduce copies to use with your staff. Remember, however, that this short, informal survey provides only a global assessment of organizational climate; it should not be used to interpret organizational functioning in each of the ten dimensions separately.

Periodically, you may decide that you want a more systematic, standardized assessment of your center's work climate, one that provides a more comprehensive analysis of organizational functioning. If so, the long version of the ECWES may suit your needs.

Formal Assessment Using the Early Childhood Work Environment Survey

The *Early Childhood Work Environment Survey* evolved from research conducted by the McCormick Center for Early Childhood Leadership at National-Louis University. The development of the ECWES was shaped by the need for an instrument that could both describe and differentiate settings along several dimensions, could demonstrate a satisfactory level of statistical reliability and validity, and could serve as a useful tool for the profession to use in monitoring and improving the quality of work life in early childhood settings.

Appendix B is a copy of the *Early Childhood Work Environment Survey*. The ECWES is copyrighted, and thus may not be reproduced to distribute to your staff. Copies may be ordered from and scored by the McCormick Center for Early Childhood Leadership. A nominal fee is charged for this computerized service. All records and results remain confidential. For further information, contact the McCormick Center for Early Childhood Leadership at National-Louis University (http://cecl.nl.edu).

Administering and scoring the ECWES. The *Early Childhood Work Environment Survey* is designed for use by all administrators, teachers, and support staff who work in a paid capacity more than 10 hours a week in a program for young children. Centers with fewer than five employees will probably find the survey less helpful because the results tend to vary only slightly with so few respondents.

This survey should be completed in private by each individual and takes approximately 15 minutes to fill out. When completed, surveys can be sent to the McCormick Center for Early Childhood Leadership for tabulation of the results. In approximately six weeks, the center will receive a Work Environment Profile summarizing the data along with an interpretation of the results.

The Work Environment Profile

Because the *Early Childhood Work Environment Survey* analyzes a center's professional environment, individuals' responses are compiled into one center profile that reflects group perceptions of current organizational practices. The profile includes information about how workers perceive the work environment, how their setting compares to what they consider to be their ideal, and how their center compares with other centers that have completed the ECWES. Here is an example of a Work Environment Profile generated from the results of one center's assessment.

> Without data, you are just another person with an opinion.
>
> *T. F. Kelly*

McCORMICK CENTER FOR EARLY CHILDHOOD LEADERSHIP
6310 Capitol Drive, Wheeling, Illinois 60090
Phone: 800/443-5522 ext. 5055   Fax: 847/465-5910
http://cecl.nl.edu

SAMPLE

WORK ENVIRONMENT PROFILE

Name: ANYWHERE CHILD CARE

Total administrative, teaching, and support staff: 15

Number of staff completing survey: 15

Date: January 1, 2010

Code: 0000

Employment pattern of respondents:

8	employed full-time (35 hours per week or more)
7	employed part-time (10-34 hours per week)
0	data not provided by respondent

PART A. STAFF'S RATINGS OF THE ORGANIZATIONAL CLIMATE (N = 15)

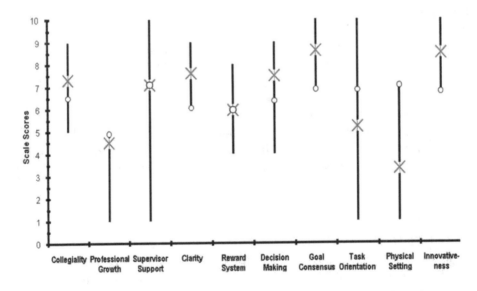

The **X** represents the average score for this dimension for subjects included in this sample.
The **O** represents the norm for this dimension based on responses of 3,980 workers in 363 centers.
The vertical line for each dimension represents the range of scores for subjects in this sample.

PART B. STAFF'S RATINGS OF THE IMPORTANCE OF EACH DIMENSION (N = 15)

Number of employees who indicated each dimension as being one of three most important to them.

3	Collegiality, co-worker relations	5	Involvement in decision making
10	Opportunities for professional growth	2	Consensus on program goals, objectives
4	Support and feedback from supervisor	2	Accomplishing work in efficient manner
3	Clarity in policies and procedures	9	Physical setting, sufficient materials
5	Equitable pay, benefits, and promotions	2	Innovativeness and creative expression

PART C. OVERALL COMMITMENT TO THE ORGANIZATION (N = 15)

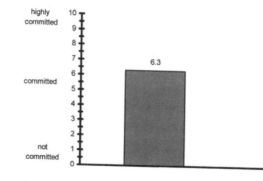

PART D. HOW THE CURRENT WORK ENVIRONMENT RESEMBLES THE IDEAL (N = 14)

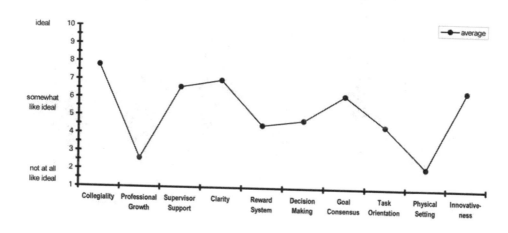

PART E. RANKING OF EDUCATIONAL GOALS AND OBJECTIVES (N = 14)

To help children develop...	Number of people who ranked item as:					
	most important					*least important*
	1	**2**	**3**	**4**	**5**	**6**
language and problem-solving skills	0	1	2	6	5	0
strong friendships, skills in sharing	3	0	4	3	2	2
concepts needed for reading and math	0	1	0	1	2	10
independence in caring for themselves	0	10	3	0	1	0
physical skill and coordination	0	1	3	4	4	2
positive self-concepts and self-esteem	11	1	2	0	0	0

PART F. TEACHERS' DECISION-MAKING INFLUENCE (N = 15)

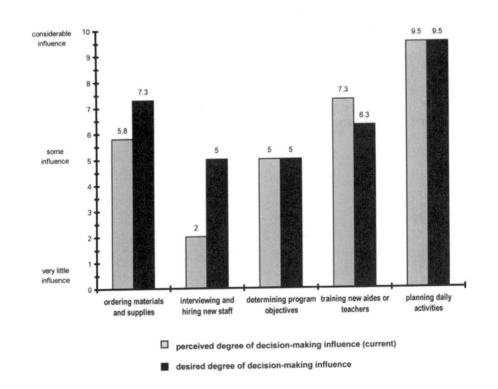

☐ perceived degree of decision-making influence (current)

■ desired degree of decision-making influence

Let's take a close look at each part of the Work Environment Profile. Even if you have used the short version of the ECWES before or designed your own survey, you will find this discussion helpful in interpreting your results.

Part A. Staff's Ratings of the Organizational Climate. This portion of the profile includes a summary of the results of questions pertaining to the ten dimensions of organizational climate. It describes the current organizational climate as measured by staff perceptions along each dimension.

To make dimension scores comparable, all scores have been standardized on a common metric. The vertical axis indicates that the lowest possible score for each dimension is 0 and the highest possible score is 10. The vertical line for each dimension indicates the range of scores (low and high) for the participating center. The circle represents the average score on this dimension for 3,980 early childhood practitioners who previously completed the *Early Childhood Work Environment Survey*. The X shows the average rating of the respondents from the participating center for each dimension.

The number of respondents' surveys used for Part A on the Work Environment Profile is indicated by the notation N = . If this number differs from the total number of staff who completed surveys, it may be because some surveys were incomplete or filled out incorrectly. Incomplete surveys are not used in the data analysis for each section. High scores in a dimension indicate that staff have generally positive perceptions of the items that comprise that dimension.

Part B. Staff's Ratings of the Importance of Each Dimension. People do not all want or expect the same things from their work environment. For some individuals, a sense of collegiality may be quite important and essential for job satisfaction. For others who prefer to work alone, the need for affiliation may be less important. Likewise, for some people, the comfort level of the physical setting and the availability of materials and supplies may be of considerable importance. For others, however, the physical setting may be minimally important.

On the ECWES, respondents are asked to indicate the three dimensions they value most highly in a work setting. The Work Environment Profile summarizes the collective importance or value that staff have assigned to each of the ten dimensions. It notes the number of employees who indicated a dimension as being one of the three most important to them.

The data summarized in Part B of the Work Environment Profile can guide a director in knowing which dimensions should be given priority in terms of attention for organizational change. In other words, administrators will achieve more lasting results in their center improvement efforts if they focus on those areas that staff rated as low in Part A and valued as high in Part B.

These measures are intended to be used as benchmarks for growth rather than hammers for change.

H. Jerome Freiberg

Looking at Part A and B together will help staff appreciate the uniqueness of their setting. Part A describes the climate as it is currently perceived by staff; Part B measures the value or importance attached to each dimension. Taken together, Part A and Part B can help staff understand how the current climate meets expectations in each area. Each center must develop its own formula for achieving a healthy organizational climate—no one prescription applies equally to all settings.

Part C. Overall Commitment to the Organization. This scale provides a summary of the staff's overall commitment to the center. Individuals who feel deeply committed to their jobs tend to put extra effort into their work and take pride in their center. This section of the profile can be read like a thermometer—the higher the bar, the stronger the collective commitment of those individuals completing the survey.

Part D. How the Current Work Environment Resembles the Ideal. Satisfaction with one's work environment can also be conceptualized as the discrepancy between current working conditions and a perceived ideal work environment. Satisfaction is greater when the discrepancy between real and ideal conditions is small. This section of the Work Environment Profile describes the composite employee perceptions of how closely their current work situation resembles their ideal work environment. This is just one additional way to understand how workers perceive present work conditions.

Part E. Ranking of Educational Goals and Objectives. There are many educational goals and objectives that guide curricular policies and procedures in early childhood programs. But the priority that staff assign to different goals may vary from one center to another. This section of the Work Environment Profile details the rank that respondents assigned to six educational objectives. If goal consensus is high at a center, the rankings for each objective will cluster. If staff have strong differences of opinion about the importance of objectives, however, the rankings will be widely dispersed.

Part F. Teachers' Decision-Making Influence. This section of the Work Environment Profile describes employees' perceptions regarding the degree of influence of the teaching staff with respect to various organizational decisions. It includes both their perceptions of the degree of teachers' *current* decision-making influence as well as their perceptions of their *desired* degree of decision-making influence.

The data summarized in this section of the profile may prove useful in understanding some of the different decisions that are typically made in early childhood programs—decisions where centralized decision making may be preferred and those where shared decision making may be possible. The appropriate balance for each center depends on the unique set of circumstances within each program and the amount of influence staff desire in each of these areas.

What Is the "Best" Climate?

A healthy, positive organizational climate is typically characterized by high energy, openness, trust, a collective sense of the ability to get things done, and a shared vision. In contrast, an unhealthy, negative work environment usually can be described as having poor communication, divisiveness, conflict, and low staff morale.

Nevertheless, each center must define its own "best" organizational climate. Just as some people prefer hot, dry weather and others like it cool and damp, the social-ecological perspective discussed in Chapter 1 helps us understand that there is no one ideal profile. Rather, each dimension must be evaluated in relation to the needs, values, and expectations of the staff and, if applicable, the board members and other administrators in each setting. The best climate is a unique blend that meets the individual and collective needs of all concerned.

Conducting a survey about organizational climate is not an end in itself, but rather the first stepping stone toward action. Simply assessing attitudes is not sufficient to increase staff morale and commitment to organizational goals. But diagnosis and evaluation of the results can give direction to your action.

A culture of accountability makes a good organization great and a great organization unstoppable.

Henry Evans

CHAPTER 3

Partly Cloudy or Partly Sunny— Viewing the World through Different Lenses

Any teacher who has worked his or her way up the ranks from classroom assistant to teacher to director will not be surprised to learn that individuals who hold different positions in the organizational hierarchy tend to view organizational climate differently. In most work settings, those in administrative positions tend to view the organization more positively than other staff members.

Research conducted at the elementary and secondary level has found that teachers' and principals' perceptions of school climate do not necessarily coincide. Teachers and administrators have different frames of reference and, consequently, different perceptions of school problems. Principals tend to view conditions more favorably than teachers. Although teachers and principals generally agree on which problems are serious, they differ considerably in their perceptions of the magnitude of those problems.

One might assume that early childhood work environments would be different. _____ _____ and secondary educational settings, a hierarchical model _____ corresponding job duties is _____ educators have long prided _____ are more egalitarian and _____ red responsibilities, and frequent _____ is the norm.

_____ tors report that they wear several _____ ram but also spending _____ alongside the teachers. Classroom _____ in the same duties, despite _____ apping domains of responsibility, _____ ould share similar perceptions of

_____ different than their elementary or _____ view the world through different _____ other times they are quite _____ asons directors may view the world _____ t the importance of expanding perspectives to appreciate differing points of view and offers concrete strategies to narrow the gap between viewpoints to achieve greater understanding.

Directors and Teachers View the World Differently

Sometimes a graphic image captures a point far better than words. Take a look at this line graph. It dramatically illustrates how teachers and administrators in early childhood settings strongly differ in the degree of their perceptions about organizational practices. Although teachers and directors generally agree on which dimensions of climate are more problematic than others, they differ considerably in their perceptions of the magnitude of those problems, with directors viewing things more positively than teachers.

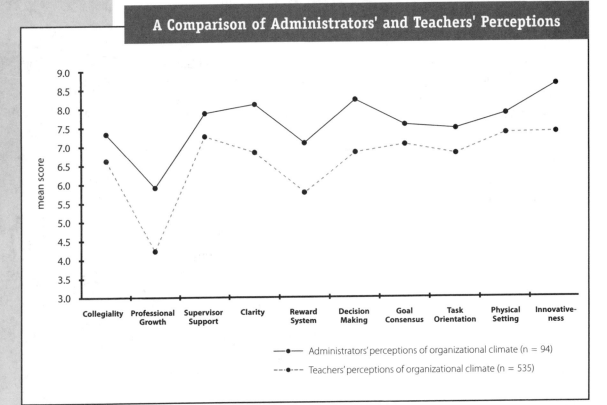

A Comparison of Administrators' and Teachers' Perceptions

—●— Administrators' perceptions of organizational climate (n = 94)

--●-- Teachers' perceptions of organizational climate (n = 535)

It is clear from the data summarized in this graph that directors consistently have a rosier picture of organizational practices than do their teachers. Why is this so? Perhaps directors see things through rose-colored glasses simply to survive the multitude of demands that come with the job. In truth, there are probably several complex and interrelated factors at work, including differences in the backgrounds of the two groups, the scope and nature of their roles, and the perceived control directors and teachers have over their jobs.

If we look at the background characteristics of administrators and teachers in early care and education programs, for example, we find significant differences in age, education, experience, salary, and professional orientation. These differences may help explain why administrators and teachers perceive the same environment differently. Everett Rogers uses the term *heterophily* to describe the existence of difference between groups of individuals. He points out that as groups become more *homophilious*, communication and understanding between them increases.

Clearly role differentiation is closely tied to perceived control. It is possible that this is why administrators as a group perceive organizational climate more favorably than teachers. Research exploring early childhood teachers' work attitudes has found that teachers generally feel they have little influence in decisions affecting center life. On paper the decision-making structure of a program may look quite egalitarian; in reality, however, teachers perceive a strong hierarchical arrangement.

Data from research using the *Early Childhood Work Environment Survey* substantiates this view. In one study, more than three-fourths of the full-time teaching staff from 421 centers report that they have less decision-making influence than they would like. Only 6% indicate that they actually have more decision-making responsibility than they would like, and less than one-fifth of the teaching staff say they have "just the right amount." Clearly there are strong differences in perceptions with respect to influence and control regarding decision making in early childhood programs.

Perception Shapes Our Sense of Reality

Okay, so differences in work attitudes have a lot to do with one's role and corresponding perspective of life at the center. But how do directors and teachers go about expanding their perspectives so they can achieve some modicum of understanding and greater appreciation for each other's point of view?

Sometimes it's fun to play around with taking different perspectives. Look at the image to the right. What do you see? Some people see a goblet or a wine glass, while others see profiles of two people facing one another.

What happens if you see only the goblet and the rest of your team sees the profiles of two people? An example like this one helps us realize how quickly we make inferences about the world using the lens we are most familiar with. If you think about it, so much of the tension we experience in our interpersonal relationships both at home and at work is because people have different perspectives from which they make inferences and draw conclusions. Our perceptions become our reality and it's hard to step out of our own limited perspective and view the world through a different set of lenses. Here's a vignette that may sound familiar.

> Margie is a very dedicated teacher in the two-year-old room. She takes pride in the special bond she has established with the children enrolled in her class. Margie is surprised when Tamara, her director, asks to meet with her about a parent complaint. Tamara informs Margie that Gabriel's mom was considering pulling him out of the program. According to Gabriel's mom, each evening when she arrives to pick up her son, he is sitting alone on a chair, wearing his jacket and waiting to go home. He appears to be downcast and bored. Gabriel's mom is worried that he is left sitting alone with nothing to do for long periods of time.
>
> Margie is stunned to hear the mother's description of the situation and quickly explains her perspective on this end-of-the-day routine. Margie says that she knows Gabriel's mom is a single parent with two children enrolled in the program. She has noticed how flustered and harried she seems at pick-up time. This is particularly true when Gabriel is busy drawing a picture and does not want to leave until it is completed to his liking. A month earlier, Gabriel even had a major temper tantrum when his mom asked him to stop drawing and get his jacket to go home. In an attempt to ease the mother's burden, Margie has Gabriel finish his activities ten minutes before pick-up time and gather up his belongings so he will be ready to go home when his mother arrives. She turns on soft, soothing music and chats with Gabriel about their day while waiting for his mom. Margie thought Gabriel's mom would be delighted with this routine.

To the ant, a few drops of rain is a flood.

Japanese Proverb

How easy it is to jump to conclusions, make assumptions, and infer intentions. Kudos to Tamara for presenting the issue to Margie in a nonjudgmental way so that she understands both sides of the story. This situation, like so many of the encounters we have every single day of our lives, reminds us that we make decisions based not so much on objective facts and information as on our perceptions of facts and information. Perceptions are powerful regulators of behavior. Taking the time to consider different perspectives can expand our understanding of why people say the things they say and do the things they do.

Three Perspectives

As you delve deeper in your thinking about perceptions, it is helpful to consider three different perspectives—*egocentric, allocentric,* and *macrocentric.* Learning to analyze situations from these different viewpoints can help you and your staff expand your understanding of human behavior and contribute to more productive work relations.

Egocentric. Egocentric perspective is our own unique point of view, shaped by our past experiences, cognitive capacity, deeply held values, and formal education. Adults are really not so different from young children in this regard; often we are guilty of narrow, egocentric thinking. We have difficulty clearly seeing someone else's point of view and perceive our perspective to be the only valid one.

Let's take a drive down the egocentric highway of life. What type of conditions do you suppose we might find? You've probably encountered more than a few egocentric drivers in your daily commute; you know the type. It's pouring rain and your windshield wipers are working overtime. You arrive at the stop sign at the same time as Mr. Egocentric, and based on the rules of the road, it is your right of way. But Mr. Egocentric pays no attention to such rules. He hydroplanes right on through the stop sign with total disregard for you as a fellow driver. Mr. Egocentric cares only about his immediate needs and has no concern for the needs of those who share the road with him.

Allocentric. An allocentric perspective takes into account another person's point of view. The root *allo* means other. An allocentric perspective allows us to experience empathy for others—to walk in their shoes and feel what they feel. Developing an allocentric perspective takes skill and patience. It involves deep listening—really trying to see the world through a different lens. As director, you can help expand your staff's allocentric capacities by asking them questions that move them out of their narrow perceptual frames.

Let's hop back in the car and see what Ms. Allocentric has to offer on the highway of life. It is a blistering hot day, the type ripe for road rage. No one wants to be sitting in their sweltering cars during rush hour traffic. Most everyone is trying to find the quickest route to get home. Horns are honking, fists are flailing, and all of sudden there is this beautiful ray of light known as Ms. Allocentric. You've been trapped in the parking lot trying to enter the line of traffic on a busy road and she is the one who stops and waves you to go ahead and pull out in front of her. Ms. Allocentric empathizes and reflects on another's point of view.

Macrocentric. Having a macrocentric perspective is being able to see the big picture—how one's actions intersect with those of others. It is like viewing the landscape from the traffic helicopter hovering above. A macrocentric perspective is not easily achieved. It requires having the capacity to be part of the picture while simultaneously being able to step outside the picture and see all the connecting elements.

Anyone driving slower than you is an idiot. Anyone driving faster than you is a maniac.

George Carlin

Let's take one final car ride to see how Mr. Macrocentric navigates the superhighway of life in the midst of a snow storm. Mr. Macrocentric is driving a big Mack truck. He sits high above all the other vehicles on the road and is an expert in driving in all sorts of weather conditions. He spends his life on the road and knows not only his own driving abilities but what to anticipate from the drivers around him. He is not in a hurry to get where he needs to go because he is fully aware of the black ice forming beneath the snow. He proceeds with caution while watching out for his fellow drivers who share the road. Mr. Macrocentric knows that a skid on black ice could impact hundreds of commuters and cause injury. He sees the big picture and takes his time as a result of this broader perspective.

As a director, you have a team wanting to put together a complex puzzle known as a quality early care and education program. Each person holds a handful of important pieces, and it is your job to take everyone's pieces and turn them into something beautiful. You are in the position of trying to articulate this macrocentric perspective to the staff in your program. The more you can help them see the big picture (the one on the lid of the puzzle box), the greater the likelihood that you'll influence and expand their perspective.

Embracing Diversity

Another valuable piece in your work to expand perspectives is diversity. You are part of a profession that has long championed the importance of promoting diversity and appreciating individual differences. Indeed, one of NAEYC's best-selling publications is *Anti-Bias Education for Young Children and Ourselves*, by Derman-Sparks and Edwards, a book devoted to helping individuals become accepting of others who are different from themselves. It is wise to take this same mindset into the administrative and staff relations arena of program operations. Respecting differing perceptions in the work world is an important step toward promoting a center climate that truly values diversity.

Our early childhood workforce is a tapestry of different races, cultures, ages, abilities, genders, religions, educational backgrounds, experiences, and lifestyles. Directors face genuine challenges in leading such a diverse set of people. One such challenge is addressing the day-to-day issues that arise when team members speak different languages, come from different cultures, hold tight to different values, and have diverse life stories. Creating a work environment that embraces this kind of diversity and celebrates contributions from all team members is a noble goal, one that takes patience and determination.

Diversity expert Judith Palmer offers three ways people typically think about diversity in the workplace:

What we see depends mainly on what we look for.

John Lubbock

- **The Golden Rule.** In this approach, you tend to view diversity as a moral issue. You welcome diversity into your program because it is the just, fair, and right thing to do.

- **Righting the Wrong.** You are focused on diversity as a legal issue and attempt to treat everyone the same.

- **Valuing Diversity.** You value differences and work to increase the awareness and acceptance of differences among your team and appreciate the value such diversity adds to the program.

The goal of the third option—valuing diversity—focuses on changing the organizational system rather than trying to change individuals. The aim is to become a truly inclusive community. Naturally, this is no small task. Perhaps Jim Greenman captured the challenge best when he said, "Diversity is the spice of life. It also makes us sneeze a lot. If we believe in it, we have to take the time to think it through for our programs."

For most groups, putting the focus on looking at daily practices and organizational systems is less threatening than directly focusing on personal attitudes and biases. People are typically more open to examining the consequences of different behaviors than putting the magnifying lens on their personal attitudes and biases. That doesn't mean attitudes and biases are ignored. To the contrary; it only means that the discussion on sensitive topics starts by looking at organizational practices and letting people reflect on their own role in promoting (or obstructing) the organization's goal of diversity in ways that are most comfortable for them.

Take the issue of gender diversity in early childhood programs. How does your program stack up in this important area? Do you have any male teachers working at your center? If so, you are clearly in the minority. Across the country, only five percent of early childhood teachers are male. Even though there is virtually unanimous agreement among early childhood practitioners and child development experts about the importance of male role models in the lives of young children, our field has been woefully unsuccessful at attracting and retaining male talent. One study found that both men and women believe our professional status and work environment would improve if there were more male teachers in the early childhood workforce.

So if your program is truly serious about promoting diversity in this area, one place to start is by examining the organizational practices that would provide evidence of this value. Eisenhauer and Pratt offer some questions to think about:

- Are photographs and posters of men engaged in caring and nurturing activities displayed for children, families, and visitors to see?

- Are picture books with positive male characters (e.g., *Lilly's Purple Plastic Purse* by Keith Henkes and *Daddy's Lullaby* by Tony Bradman) available in the classroom?

- Are men invited to volunteer in the classroom?

- Are men represented on your center's advisory board?

- Is gender-neutral language used in your center's descriptive literature?

- Do your job vacancy announcements promote the importance of gender diversity in your program?

What is interesting about this list is that you could use these same ideas to promote the acceptance of other types of diversity. Display photographs and posters of people with differing abilities, select picture books with positive images from various cultures and invite grandparents from the community to volunteer in the classroom. The focus is on being mindful about promoting the acceptance of diversity. Once again, in your role as a leader you have an opportunity to put into place organizational systems that value diversity. In the following table Margie Carter offers additional elements to consider.

Examining Organizational Diversity

- Stay current and keep deepening your knowledge about your context, the backgrounds of the children, families, and staff.

- Create opportunities for exchanges around values, assumptions, hopes, and dreams with the children's families and among the staff.

- Examine your paper work, your language, and your approach to communicating with people. Change systems that make people invisible or suggest that only one cultural perspective, language, or family structure is normal.

- Devote time to developing a positive approach to living with and negotiating differences. Practice regularly managing conflicts around simple issues before you are faced with the complex, hot ones.

From Carter, M. (2004, May/June). Tolerance or transformation: What's our training goal? *Exchange*, 22–24. Reprinted with permission.

The Study Circles Resource Center, a project of the Topsfield Foundation, provides a terrific guide to help you structure meaningful conversations among your team. Here are some questions to get you started:

Who are we? A beginning step toward embracing diversity is sharing our own stories and experiences and exploring a basic question: Why do we describe ourselves and others in so many different ways? By sharing stories, we discover how diverse experiences have shaped us, divided us, and linked us. Through this dialogue, you may come to understand each member of your center just a little bit better.

What are our bonds and boundaries? When people don't feel welcome or comfortable, when they feel they're being cut out or threatened, it affects the spirit of the entire program. Learning how our actions or attitudes affect each other prepares us to imagine what it would take to create a better life together. At one time or another, every person has felt like an outsider. Draw on that experience in thinking about the signs that say you belong and the ones that say you don't.

What ties us together? Conversations about what matters to us help us understand our respective experiences and our hopes for the future. Through telling our stories and sharing our ideas and life experiences, we can find common ground.

Closing the Gap

What does all this mean for directors interested in improving the climate of their centers? First and foremost, it suggests that administrators and teachers cannot assume that their view of center life is necessarily a shared one. Whether differences in perception arise from differences in culture and background, from the structure of roles and responsibilities, or from the perceived control associated with roles, it is clear that individuals do filter their perceptions of organizational practices through a lens related to their position in the center.

A mismatch between directors' and teachers' perceptions can have a detrimental effect on the quality of work life for everyone. Identifying where perceptions differ is the first step in structuring opportunities to promote the convergence of viewpoints. Help your team engage in learning conversations that explore differing perspectives.

A learning conversation begins with the premise that we each have something to gain from hearing the other person's opinions on an issue. "Share with me your feelings about this issue" or "Help me understand your perspective regarding this situation" are good ways to launch a learning conversation. Here are some additional suggestions for closing the gap.

One of the hardest tasks of leadership is understanding that you are not what you are, but what you are perceived to be by others.

Edward Flom

41

- Look for every opportunity to help individuals frame a situation from a different point of view. For example, at a staff meeting when someone is absent, you might say, "Jason isn't able to be with us today. How do you think he would feel about the group's decision to change the lunch schedule?"

- Whenever disagreements between teachers occur, encourage a frank, open discussion about different points of view. Help the parties understand that one person doesn't have to be wrong for the other one to be right—that we all have a piece of the truth and that truth is usually shaped by the way we interpret the information we have. Help the individuals untangle intent and impact. We infer intentions from the impact that an action has on us, and frequently we assume the worst. It is only through a learning conversation that we can really understand someone's intent.

- Facilitate a discussion about the events in people's lives that have resulted in a major shift in their perspective about the world. Common events might include going off to college, getting married, becoming a parent, being diagnosed with a life-threatening illness, or experiencing the death of a loved one. The discussion will inevitably lead to additional examples of life-changing events that were shared by many, like 9/11 and Hurricane Katrina.

- Look for opportunities to share examples of how your own assumptions, beliefs, and behavior have changed as you have gotten older and broadened your range of experiences. Also, whenever possible, share the rationale for the decisions you make to help staff see the big picture of interconnected parts in administrating a program.

- Track down resources like *Seeing Double* or *The Great Book of Optical Illusions* to find examples of optical brainteasers. Share some playful examples at a staff meeting to reinforce the point that the reality in which we live is based on our different perspectives.

- Start a book club at your center with the focus on selections about individuals who have gone through life-changing events and personal enlightenment. Alternatively, select books that describe different cultures or tell stories about tolerance and reconciliation of different points of view.

Closing the gap made by differences in perceptions and laying the foundation for a more competent system, one in which everyone can articulate core beliefs and the shared purpose of their work, is a big step toward improving the organizational climate in your program.

CHAPTER 4

Changing the Weather— The Director's Role

In life, you have no real control over the weather. You wake up in the morning and look out your window or listen to the local meteorologist for guidance on how to dress. You probably also prepare for the unexpected. You pack an umbrella in case there's a sudden cloudburst, or you bring along a light jacket just in case a cold front sweeps in. As the leader of an early childhood program, however, you have tremendous influence on the weather in your center.

Your role in the organization is central and complex. In a number of powerful ways, you shape your center as a workplace. Each action or decision you make, big or small, has a way of reverberating through the center. This chapter explores how you can lead the way to excellence by communicating with purpose, dealing with conflict, nurturing a culture of inquiry, and instilling norms of continuous improvement. All these leadership actions help clear the fog and create a positive work climate.

Communicating with Purpose

Do you ever feel like one of the adults from the comic strip *Charlie Brown*? They were invisible and their communication always sounded the same: "Woh-woh-woh." Communication is an elusive concept that involves a circular process of sharing one's ideas and feelings with others and interpreting their feedback. In many ways, effective leadership in early care and education is synonymous with effective communication because the success of a program relies so heavily on the open, honest exchange of information, ideas, and feelings. Good communication is the lubricating oil that makes all parts of an operation run smoothly and helps create a great place to work.

When thinking about communication, it is useful to consider two aspects—the different modes of communicating information that you use and your tone and style. You can think metaphorically of these two components as the body and soul of effective communication. Let's dig deeper.

Modes of communication. Consider for a moment all the different ways you communicate information to your teachers and parents—hallway conversations, informal memos, quick phone calls, e-mails, and notes posted on the bulletin board, among others. One thing is for certain: when directors are not deliberate in the mode they want information communicated and don't have established systems in place for communicating different types of information, the proverbial grapevine will surely fill the gap.

At centers where communication channels are weak, teachers often remark that they are the last to know about a new procedure or an event that has been planned. They feel they receive too many memos and they don't know which ones are important. They complain they are bombarded with too much verbal information when they are at staff meetings or when they are preoccupied doing something else. Likewise, directors report they are equally frustrated because they have to repeat directions several times. They get annoyed when important information is ignored.

The first step toward improving communication in your program is to assess how information is communicated vertically and horizontally through the center. Once this is done, you may find it easier to devise more streamlined methods that highlight important information on a regular and anticipated basis. Essential to this task is determining what kind of information is best communicated in verbal form and what kind of information is best disseminated in written form. Take a moment now to complete Exercise 4.

Exercise 4

Read through the list below and check the different modes of communication you use to keep staff informed:

☐ Small- and large-group meetings   ☐ Voicemail

☐ Hallway conversations   ☐ Text messaging

☐ In-house newsletter   ☐ Website, Twitter, or Facebook

☐ Internal memos   ☐ Daily message log

☐ E-mail   ☐ Routing slips

☐ Staff bulletin board   ☐ Other _____

Looking over the different modes of communication you checked, think about how you could communicate something more efficiently by changing the mode you use. For example, if you currently spend meeting time updating your staff about board decisions, you might distribute this information in written form for folks to read before the meeting. This step can free up meeting time for other more pressing issues. What are some other examples of how you might communicate information more efficiently?

_____

_____

_____

Protecting staff and parents from information overload is important in an age when computers and photocopy machines make it easy to generate mountains of letters, memos, and reports in very little time. It's easy to get buried under a paper avalanche.

It is also important to note that the people on your team have their own preferred modes of communication. Periodically ask your teachers, your support staff, and even your board, if you have one, how they prefer to receive different kinds of information. For some employees, e-mail is the best way. For others, an e-mail message may sit in their electronic inbox untouched for days. They might benefit more from a voicemail message or a paper memo in their in-box.

While individualizing is important, there must also be a healthy balance, so you do not make more work for yourself. It is important to create communication streams that are efficient for both the sender and the receivers. Through conversations, you can determine which modes are most efficient for your staff as a whole.

Creating a system in which certain kinds of written information are communicated in a regular and anticipated way is the first step in coping with communication clutter. Some directors, for example, distribute a Monday Morning Memo (always printed on the same color paper to distinguish it from other notes) that summarizes important information teachers need for the week. This could include information about field trips planned, forms due, or observations scheduled. Sending out your center's newsletter on the same day each month is a way that parents can anticipate communication.

Tone and style. "Don't use that tone of voice with me, young lady!" Perhaps a voice from childhood harkens back as you consider communication concepts of tone and style. Tone is a manner of speaking or writing that conveys a certain attitude. Do you project an attitude of "We are all in this together" or "It's my way or the highway"? Do you use the terms *we* and *our* in your everyday language? These subtle messages send a clear signal to those in your work environment. Your communication style is the specific way you craft and deliver your words, including pace, volume, and inflection, as well as your gestures and overall body language. Some people are very direct in their style; others are more spirited, analytical, or considerate in their interpersonal interactions. How would you characterize your communication style?

In his book, *The Secret Language of Leadership*, Stephen Denning says that while it is true that a leader's actions will eventually speak louder than words, in the short run, it's what leaders say—or don't say—that delivers the emotional impact in the message. The right words can have a galvanizing effect, generating enthusiasm, energy, momentum and more, while the wrong words can undermine the best intentions and kill initiative stone dead on the spot.

Good communication skills can be learned and deliberately applied. Here are some things you can do to achieve the positive communication outcomes you are looking for:

- Recognize the power of every conversation you have. Your tone of optimism or defeatism creates expectations for your staff. If you aren't positive and hopeful, why should they be?

- Be authentic in your conversations. The best leaders talk *with* people, not *at* them.

- Help your staff understand that the way they talk to one another is as important as what they talk about. Courtesy and respect are the hallmarks of a caring collegial environment.

- Model positive intentionality by always presuming that others' motives and intentions are honorable.

- Begin each interaction with the end in mind. Ask yourself what you want to accomplish in an exchange with another person. If you have a clear idea in your own mind of the result you want by the end of a conversation, e-mail message, or memo, it will help you structure your comments more concisely.

- Avoid generalities when describing people or things. There is a real temptation to rely on vague words like *good, bad, sometimes*, and *mostly* to describe things. Also, be mindful of the educational jargon you use. You may have a clear understanding of what you mean when you say *child-centered, accountable,* or *developmentally appropriate*, but the families and teachers with whom you are speaking may not have the same understanding. Vague words and phrases are open to misinterpretation. Try to give specific examples to illustrate what you say.

- Keep the other person's perspective in mind as you frame your comments. Most people operate on a WIFM (What's In It For Me?) wavelength. Thinking from the other person's perspective helps you structure your message in a more persuasive way.

- Be concise; try not to over-communicate. Don't be guilty of trying to convey too much information (TMI) or using too many words (TMW). Be short and sweet, as they say. Rambling can be a liability in your quest to win friends and influence people.

- Check your tone. It is not what you say but how you say it that usually determines how others interpret what you have said.

- Make your words and body language congruent. Personal mannerisms—gestures, eye contact, sitting or standing position, and other expressive features—carry powerful messages that can strengthen or weaken what you hope to communicate.

- Be aware of how background noise and distractions, as well as the placement of furniture, can affect communication. A desk, seating arrangement, or a poorly positioned table can all be barriers to communication.

- Respect the importance of good timing. Your message may be on target, but if the timing isn't right, you may strike out.

Most important, communicate in ways that show that you value people. It is said that people don't care how much you know until they know how much you care. Everyone wants to feel special and significant.

Life strategist Dr. Phil McGraw is fond of saying that the number one need among all people is acceptance and the number one fear among all people is rejection. There may not be actual empirical evidence to back up that claim, but the point is still valid—your tone and style can help bolster a person's self-esteem or slowly erode it. So ask yourself: Do my words and actions generate a sense that each person at the center is a valued and significant member of the organization?

Of course, talking is only half the equation in good communication. Of equal importance is learning to be an empathic, attentive listener. Active listening is difficult. Our minds tend to race ahead and think of what we are going to say next, or we get sidetracked by wandering thoughts. As Stephen Covey reminds us, "The deepest hunger of the human soul is to be understood. The deepest hunger of the human body is for air. If you can listen to another person, in depth, until they feel understood, it's the equivalent of giving them air."

I remind myself every morning: Nothing I say this day will teach me anything. So if I'm going to learn, I must do it by listening.

Larry King

Dealing with Conflict

The field of early care and education is filled with caring, compassionate people. And some of those people are just too caring, too compassionate, and too doggone nice. Is that possible? Perhaps that is an oversimplification; but it is fair to say that in many programs there are staff who are not comfortable dealing with differences of opinion. They are squeemish about conflict and avoid at all costs encounters with those who hold different viewpoints. They'd like to just sweep those differences and disagreements right under that cozy circle-time rug. Nice thought, but when differences are not dealt with, even minor disagreements and petty annoyances can seed the storm clouds producing gale-force winds that can undermine a program's operation.

So how do you address conflict in the workplace? If you've been a director for even a short time, no doubt you've experienced a day or two when conflict came knocking at your door. Much time can be spent dealing with conflicts around work ethics, educational philosophy, interpersonal relationships, and cultural differences.

On the one hand, you want staff to be comfortable sharing their frustrations with you. On the other hand, you don't want to fall into the trap of being personally responsible for fixing every conflict that arises in the center. Let's consider a conflict resolution approach to promote open, direct communication in your organization.

Quality early childhood programs teach young children problem solving skills. How many times have you heard teachers tell children to use their words? Yet, often adults avoid confronting issues with co-workers. For some people, just hearing the word *conflict* brings up immediate negative feelings. Yet, highly charged differences of opinion are a normal and potentially healthy aspect of any workplace.

Being able to embrace conflicting ideas means you perceive the process and end result of conflict as positive. Through conflict, misinterpretations can be clarified. Through conflict, what you thought was a good idea can become even better. And when handled professionally, through conflict we actually come to better understandings of one another.

A valuable tool in creating a climate for open, direct communication is offered by Roger Fisher and William Ury in *Getting to Yes: Negotiating Agreement without Giving In*. Their book offers a concise, step-by-step strategy for addressing conflict in the workplace. Fisher and Ury offer four principles of negotiation: separate the people from the problem; focus on interests, not positions; invent options for mutual gain; and insist on using objective criteria. Let's explore each of these concepts.

Separate the people from the problem. When people are in conflict, emotions run high. Out of fear or frustration, it is easy to want to personally attack the

Leaders do not avoid, repress, or deny conflict, but rather see it as an opportunity.

Warren Bennis

other person. It is important to remember, however, that in any conflict, both parties have deeply held values, different backgrounds, and points of view. Conflict resolution begins by clarifying each person's perceptions of the situation and the underlying values or beliefs that are prompting specific behaviors.

Focus on interests, not positions. According to Fisher and Ury, the basic problem in a negotiation lies not in conflicting positions, but in the conflict between each side's needs, desires, concerns, and fears. Desires and concerns are interests. Interests motivate people. Your position is something you have decided. Your interests are what caused you to decide. Focusing on interests instead of positions leads to solutions.

Invent options for mutual gain. Fisher and Ury encourage brainstorming as an effective strategy for generating mutually acceptable options. They share the tale of two sisters fighting over an orange. After agreeing to divide the orange in half, the first sister takes her half, eats the fruit, and throws away the peel; the other sister throws away the fruit and uses the peel from her half in baking a cake. Too many negotiations end up with half an orange for each side instead of the whole fruit for one and the whole peel for the other. After a variety of proposals have been made, the parties can begin to evaluate ideas.

Insist on using objective criteria. The final step in the conflict-resolution process is to commit to reaching a solution based on principle, not pressure. This can be done by developing objective criteria. Frame each issue as a joint search for objective criteria. Be open to discussing which criteria are most appropriate and how they should be applied.

Here is an example of how one program successfully resolved a conflict:

> Michelle, a preschool teacher, came into her director Joann's office and slammed the door behind her. Her arms tightly folded and tapping her foot, she was clearly furious and on the verge of tears. She exclaimed, "That's it. I have had it! I can't work another day with Kelly! You have to do something about her. She is useless in the classroom. She always expects me to do the dirty work, like clean out the paint cups, soak the brushes, and wash down the tables and chairs. It's all on my shoulders! You need to talk to her or move me to a different room. I'm tired of her lazy attitude."
>
> Joann could tell that Michelle clearly valued a clean, orderly classroom environment. She wanted to hear Kelly's position on the issue, so she set up a meeting to address the conflict between the two teachers. She asked Michelle and Kelly to each describe their perception of the current problem. Kelly explained that she was working hard to foster nurturing relationships with children,

especially since it was the start of a new school year. Taking time away from interactions to clean was less important to her.

By facilitating this meeting Joann felt she was able to help the two teachers see one another's perspectives and express their deeply held values. Obviously both values were important in creating a quality program for children.

Her next step was to determine whether Michelle and Kelly had any shared interests. Did they have common goals for the children and families in their classroom? How might those interests lead to a solution about keeping the classroom clean? Perhaps a shared interest was having the classroom be a place where children and their parents feel welcomed and want to spend time.

A quick-and-easy solution might have been for Kelly to simply agree to help more often with cleaning the classroom. However, by investing time in brainstorming, other options and solutions emerged. Joann found that the two teachers actually enjoyed thinking outside the box. Some of their ideas included paying the cleaning service more to do additional maintenance or assigning a parent volunteer the art cleanup task. These were obviously not quick or easy-to-implement solutions, but the very act of brainstorming created a sense of working collaboratively to solve the problem rather than pointing fingers at one another.

Joann had Michelle and Kelly turn to the NAEYC accreditation criteria and the revised Early Childhood Environment Rating Scale (ECERS-R) as possible criteria for guiding their decision making. Using objective criteria certainly took some of the emotion out of the situation. Both of these sources provided a sound rationale for the importance of maintaining a clean, healthy learning environment. But they also stressed the importance of promoting positive relationships with children and parents.

In the end, Kelly agreed to be more conscientious in keeping the room clean and Michelle felt validated for the important contribution she made in maintaining an orderly environment. Their conversations, however, yielded something even more powerful in strengthening this teaching team. Michelle expressed her feeling that she was not entirely comfortable talking with the parents and acknowledged Kelly's strength in this area. They agreed to have Kelly assume a more prominent role in family relations. Moving forward, they would each be more mindful of the other's values and find new ways to support one another.

As early childhood educators, we value individuality among children by embracing their unique perspectives and dispositions. Yet, as adults, we grapple with such differences in the workplace. "If only Kelly could be more like me. If only she did things the way I do them or valued the things I value, we would get along just fine." Isn't that what Michelle was implying?

By applying the four principles of negotiation offered by Fisher and Ury, Joann was able to model for her teachers how to find common ground and resolve conflicts. It is important to remember that the teachers and support staff in your program have different abilities, needs, values, and expectations. In creating a safe process to openly discuss differences, you establish a work place built on mutual trust and respect for one another.

Cultivating a Culture of Inquiry

Have you ever calculated the number of hours a week that teachers get to interact with one another as professional colleagues? You may have a monthly staff meeting or an occasional centerwide event that brings the entire team together, but in most centers, interactions between teachers are brief and infrequent—a quick hallway conversation before the children arrive, whispered tones during naptime, or a hurried summary of the day's events as teachers head out the door to go home.

If you are truly committed to creating a great place to work, then rethink the amount of time teachers spend isolated behind their classroom doors. Consider what steps you might take to build a professional learning community that fosters a culture of inquiry and adult learning.

In a professional learning community, teachers are brought together because of their dedication to children's learning and a corresponding desire to better understand matters of teaching and learning. The goal is to examine individual children's work based on observation notes and documentation in order to better accommodate their individual needs and extend learning. Over time, what develops is a set of shared beliefs about effective instructional practices and a unified approach to addressing challenging problems that arise in the classroom.

Early childhood author Margie Carter believes strongly that a central role of directors should be developing teachers' confidence, voice, and integrity. When teachers see themselves as researchers and their classrooms as laboratories for investigating human development, their professional orientation is strengthened and they feel empowered.

Developing an organizational climate that promotes adult learning is a powerful way to genuinely influence and inspire others. Carter states that beyond networking, the purpose of a learning community is to engage in a disciplined dialogue to uncover the possible significance of teachers' documentation of children's play and learning, and the implications for their teaching.

Quality is never an accident. It is always the result of high intention, sincere effort, intelligent direction, and skillful execution. It represents the wise choice of many alternatives.

William A. Foster

The way professional learning communities are implemented varies according to the context of each situation. In many centers, a 30- to 45-minute block of time is set aside each week for the teachers in three or four classrooms to meet. At each meeting, a teacher presents documentation collected on one child and poses a series of questions to colleagues. The purpose of the session is not to critique, offer advice, or discuss the past with questions like "Why didn't you...?" but rather to brainstorm and pose questions that will help the teacher reflect on next steps to build on the child's interests and achieve the desired learning outcome.

In some settings these conversations are facilitated by a lead teacher, mentor, or supervisor. In other settings, teachers are trained in how to provide peer support and they rotate the role of serving as facilitator. Whatever the structure, the power of these collaborative conversations resides in the fact that teachers begin to share publicly the thoughts and reflections they have traditionally held privately.

Ann Pelo writes, "Early childhood programs ought to be incubators of inquiry. Children, teachers, families, and program administrators, collectively and individually engaged in systematic investigation, searching and researching, asking questions, mulling over hypotheses, debating, and trying on new perspectives." Parker Palmer adds that people have inside them the resources necessary to deal with their own problems if only we can create a safe space for them to hear what their inner teaching is trying to tell them. This means that groups need to develop the habit of being together "without fixing, saving, advising, or setting each other straight."

Your prospects for improving program quality grow when you take deliberate steps to reduce isolation of teaching teams and build a comprehensive learning community. Think of how you might modify work schedules and staffing patterns to carve out more time for teachers to plan together, observe each other's classrooms, and meet regularly to talk about teaching strategies and their experiences with children. As you begin to develop your own vision of what this might mean for your program, reflect on the following questions:

- What shared problems, goals, or interests might bring your teachers together?

- How can you configure time and space to support frequent and focused communication among teachers?

- What topics might invigorate opportunities for extended collaboration?

- What resources could you provide to support a learning community in making good use of professional development, networking opportunities, or new technologies?

Shifts toward a Successful Learning Community

How will you know when you've achieved an authentic learning community? There are three critical cultural shifts that will let you know you are on the right track.

- **A shift in fundamental purpose from teaching to learning.** When program staff passionately and sincerely adopt the goal of supporting children's development, they are driven to pursue fundamentally different questions and work in profoundly different ways. The focus changes from *teaching* (what teachers do) to *learning* (how children grow and change as a result of what teachers do).

- **A shift in the work of teachers.** Learning communities recognize that there is little hope of helping children in their development unless those within the center work collaboratively to accomplish that fundamental purpose. A teacher's world can change when the center shifts from a culture of isolation to a culture of collaboration.

- **A shift in focus.** Educators in learning communities realize that they will not know if their collaborative efforts to help all children in preparing for school success have been successful without a focus on results. They are hungry for evidence to respond to children who need additional support as well as to inform and improve their own professional practice. Their focus shifts from input to outcome and from intentions to results.

Adapted from DuFour, R. (2004, May). What is a "professional learning community"? *Educational Leadership, 61*(8), 6–11.

Instilling Norms of Continuous Improvement

No doubt about it—quality is a moving target! What we once thought of as best practices have become standard practices. There always seems to be new and improved practices with higher benchmarks of excellence. When staff recognize that expectations of quality change and understand that the idea of continuous improvement is not just about them, the center benefits.

So how do you imbue teachers with the spirit to keep improving, to continue to grow, and to improve professional practices? It all starts with you, the leader. Creating norms of continuous improvement is really a mindset, a way of thinking about achieving and sustaining organizational effectiveness. Some teachers will readily embrace this concept (they're usually the ones who also set new personal goals each year) while others do so begrudgingly.

In our society, we celebrate those who make bold, grand changes, taking on monumental tasks or implementing ground-breaking, innovative initiatives. But this radical mindset serves only to heighten fear. Fortunately, there are other ways to approach change. In the Japanese culture, there is a concept referred to as *kaizen*. Kaizen emphasizes taking small, doable steps in any change process, personal or organizational. Approaching change from this perspective helps eliminate the fear and resistance that are byproducts of the change process. By breaking down change into small incremental steps, improvements seem more achievable while the ultimate goal remains great.

There is a terrific story of one program's journey toward improvement that models kaizen. This center's physical environment was considered an eyesore. There were many large-scale needs including the center's overall dilapidated appearance, overgrown shrubs, weeds sprouting in the sidewalk, and broken equipment and furniture. The director and teachers opted for a small, doable change that was highly visible to everyone in the work environment—the staff restrooms! They put on a coat of fresh paint and added pictures, mirrors, and plants. They created a "pamper yourself" corner with a candle, assorted lotions, and toiletries. They posted inspirational quotes. The restroom renovation sent a message that change was possible and inspired other members of the program to participate in future changes. After achieving this smaller task, staff were not as intimidated by the idea of taking on all the other changes to the physical environment that were needed.

Taking small steps toward change makes sense when deciding where to begin improving the organizational climate in your center. As the director of your program, you deal with a wide range of issues every day. You are the gatekeeper of quality, setting the expectations for others to follow. Your role is pivotal to program success. Without efficient and effective systems in place at the organizational level, quality teaching practices cannot be sustained at the classroom level.

Using the ten dimensions of organizational climate as a basis for program improvement may seem like a daunting task. But following the kaizen approach and making small incremental changes can help reduce feelings of anxiety, encourage creativity, and increase effectiveness. By choosing one dimension to work on and crafting an action plan, you are taking an important step in creating a norm of continuous improvement at your center and helping achieve your goal of improving the quality of work life.

CHAPTER 5

Ten Ways to Guarantee a Bright Forecast

Chances are you selected this book because you genuinely want to create a great place to work. You want to know how you as chief weather forecaster can help ensure bright and sunny days ahead. Well, hold on to your hat. We're about to take a whirlwind tour of each dimension of organizational climate to look at different strategies you can begin to implement today that will increase your teachers' self-confidence, competence in the classroom, and commitment to the organization.

Nurture that Collegial Spirit

The men and women who enter the field of early care and education are caring and dedicated educators. But the treadmill of activity that consumes their time and energy on the job can keep them from establishing close relationships with one another. The physical layout of space, time pressures, and conflicting schedules are just some of the barriers that prevent teachers from exchanging information, sharing ideas, and lending and receiving support.

As director, you play an instrumental role in encouraging your teachers to support each other and in nurturing a collegial spirit. When a deep sense of collegiality exists in a group, it inspires enthusiasm, devotion, and a strong regard for the honor of the group. Sounds like the sort of thing everyone would like to see in their program, right? But wise directors know they can't force a sense of esprit de corps. Contrived collegiality invariably backfires. A genuine sense of collegiality must be nurtured and developed by careful attention to the social and affiliation needs of people who work together.

One way you can begin to sow the seeds of collegiality is to help surface the qualities that your staff feel are important in their co-workers. Appendix C, "I Value a Co-Worker Who Is...", is a handout you can use at a staff meeting for just this purpose. This activity should spark an interesting dialogue about the various attributes that can help promote collegiality among your team.

You might also consider guiding your staff to develop a collegial contract that can serve as their commitment to establish and maintain open, honest, and trusting relationships with one another. We've included a sample contract, "Commitment to My Colleagues," developed by the director of a large hospital-based program.

As your colleague, with a shared goal of providing outstanding child care services, I commit to the following.

I will:

- admit when I make a mistake and be honest about what I need to do to prevent the same mistake in the future.
- not engage in the B's (bickering and backbiting).
- not complain about another team member to you. If I hear you doing so, I will ask you to talk to that team member.
- accept you as you are today and forget and forgive past problems.
- follow the Golden Rule: "Do unto others as I wish others to do unto me."
- respect your ideas by listening to them and talking about them with you.
- never harbor resentment. If we do disagree, we will come to the best possible outcome. I will not hold a grudge against you for having different ideas.
- trust you with my personal and professional material possessions.
- greet you with a smile and warm hello each time I see you.
- help you with your job when I can and when I am needed.
- remember that neither of us is perfect, and that human errors are opportunities, not for shame or guilt but for forgiveness and growth.

I will affirm my commitment to the mission of our center by taking part in the following activities.

I will:

- commit to finding solutions to problems rather than complaining about them or blaming someone for them.
- make every attempt to create a fun and enjoyable workplace by adding a sense of humor to the work environment.
- use the center's materials wisely and always put things back when finished with my shift.
- report any errors to the appropriate supervisor and not place blame when something goes wrong at the center.

In addition to my commitment to the above, I have read NAEYC's Code of Ethical Conduct and agree that I will follow the code to the best of my ability.

_____   _____

Employee Signature   Date

Developed by Joleen Patton, Director of Blessing Hospital Child Care Center, Quincy, IL.

Also, think about your center's physical layout and staffing schedules. Are these barriers that prevent teachers from establishing supportive work relationships? Is there anything you can change about the physical layout or your staffing patterns that would promote greater collaboration among teachers? Here are a few more ways to promote healthy co-worker relations at your program:

- Keep your staff roster up-to-date and distribute a staff birthday list.

- Schedule an occasional potluck breakfast or dinner, or host a "happy hour" on Friday afternoons where staff can talk about the things that made them smile during the week.

- Ask two or more teachers to work together on a special project, such as a parent meeting or end-of-the-year picnic.

- Adjust work schedules to encourage carpooling.

- Make a dedicated space for staff to meet, prepare materials, and talk without disruption.

- Encourage joint field trips or curriculum projects that include several classrooms.

- Schedule an annual weekend retreat where staff can get together (without their spouses and children) to establish and renew relationships.

A note about new staff. Pay special attention during the first few days of a new employee's integration into your program. Welcome new teachers and support staff warmly as part of your work family and set them up with a "buddy" on their first day. Plan a systematic orientation to cover information new staff members need during their first day, first week, and first month of employment. Experienced teachers can take an active role in orienting and mentoring new teachers.

Another way to nurture collegiality is to become intentional about rituals and celebrations. Leadership authors Lee Bolman and Terrance Deal have written extensively on this topic. They say, "Rituals and celebrations

"They meet in there. Some kind of support group."

help us experience unseen webs of significance that tie a community together. There may be grand celebrations for special occasions, but organizations also need simple rituals that infuse meaning and purpose into daily routine. Without rituals and celebrations, transitions become incomplete, a clutter of comings and goings. Life becomes an endless set of Wednesdays."

What rituals and celebrations do you have at your center to keep work life from seeming like an endless set of Wednesdays? When woven genuinely into the life of the program, you'll find that simple rituals and celebrations provide a sense of renewal, reinforce bonds between people, and provide opportunities to enjoy life's deeper meaning. So find reasons to celebrate and begin to create fun rituals and traditions that bring smiles to people's faces.

Finally, on a lighter note, you may want to assess how laughter is (or isn't) an integral part of the life of your center. Have you created a climate where fun is encouraged, where spontaneous moments of humor are celebrated? If you are serious about pumping up the fun factor in the program and injecting some levity into the workplace, here are some things you might try:

- Designate one bulletin board as a place for staff to post cartoons, jokes, and humourous photos.

- Attach a cartoon or a short joke to the memos you distribute.

- Institute a Crazy Hairdo Day, an Ugly Sweater Day, or an Outrageous Outfit Day. Award joke prizes for winners.

- Host a daytime pajama party where all the children and teachers wear their pajamas.

- Use fun props like Slinkies, Koosh Balls, a Magic 8-Ball, the Easy Button, or Silly Putty during staff meetings to add a bit of levity.

Implement High-Impact Professional Development

In Chapter 4 we introduced the concept of a learning community, stressing the point that when a program fosters a culture of inquiry, teachers play an important role in shaping the agenda for their own learning. If you are successful at creating a vibrant learning environment for the adults in your center, then they will be better equipped to offer stimulating and engaging learning experiences for the children in their care. Put simply, it is the adults who need to be the focus of your attention.

The operative phrase in the heading of this section is *high-impact*. You want the professional development experiences that teachers take part in to be high impact—relevant, engaging, and immediately applicable to their classroom setting. But you also

Sometimes we must make a serious effort to be frivolous.

Erma Brombeck

want to ensure that the training that teachers receive has a high impact on the children in their care. That means that an integral part of the center's staff development plan needs to include information about how to assess educational outcomes for young children. Teachers need to see the connection between their efforts and the educational outcomes of the children in their care. As Douglas Reeves states, "High-impact learning requires a radical transformation from transmission to focus and deliberate practice."

Providing ample opportunities for professional development is important in any educational setting, but it is particularly crucial in early care and education because of the increased attention on professional standards in our field. The provision of professional development must not be haphazard; too much is at stake.

Even on a limited budget, there are many ways you can increase opportunities for staff to expand their knowledge base and develop new skills and competencies. Some programs provide release time for teachers to observe master teachers in action. Others pay registration fees for staff to attend workshops or educational conferences. Not only do these activities rejuvenate teachers, but the benefits are multiplied when teachers return and share the new information and resources with other staff. Below is a sample form you can ask teachers to complete after attending a workshop or conference.

Professional Development Feedback

Name: _____

Session title: _____

Date: _____

Presented by: _____

Two things I learned that I am eager to share with my colleagues:

1. _____

2. _____

Two great ideas I plan to implement:

1. _____

2. _____

Two outcomes I hope will result from my efforts:

1. _____

2. _____

Many directors lament that they don't have the financial resources to hire substitutes to cover for teachers to attend training off-site or to pay for specialists to provide training on-site. But the research shows that the emphasis centers place on professional development activities seems to be tied more to managerial priorities than to real financial constraints. Directors experiencing the same economic and financial headwinds can have very strong staff development plans. They have learned that professional growth opportunities need not be limited to special occasions. Instead, a good staff development plan weaves growth opportunities into the daily life of the center. Here are some things you can do:

- Begin each staff meeting with a few minutes for teachers to share a new resource or curriculum idea with others.

- Invite professors from local colleges to talk about their research or topics relating to child development, instructional strategies, assessment, or working with children with special needs.

- Encourage teachers to observe one another and work together to refine their teaching practices.

- Maintain a professional library where staff can check out books, journals, or curriculum resources or view DVDs about different early childhood issues.

The key to successful staff development is individualizing training needs to the experience level and career stage of each person. The underlying assumption is that each person progresses personally and professionally along a developmental path. Each stage has characteristics that make it distinct from preceding and subsequent levels. The kinds of concerns, capabilities, and perspectives teachers have at one stage are not the same as those of teachers at different stages of experience and training. No single training approach will work for all teachers. If professional development is to be meaningful, it must be tailored to the needs of individual teachers.

Don't forget that your own behavior interacting with parents and children also serves as a source of professional development for your teachers. Although you may not be involved with the children every day, by making it a point to use the kind of behaviors and interactions you expect from your teachers, you demonstrate through your actions the expectations you have for your program. Your willingness to pitch in to assist during a sudden staff shortage, a field trip, or other situation gives you the opportunity to show skilled interactions with children, families, and other teachers.

Your active involvement in professional organizations also indicates your commitment to your own growth and sets an example for what is expected of staff. Some centers pay membership fees for teachers to belong to NAEYC or other professional associations. Think about giving a gift subscription to a professional journal for a special birthday or employment anniversary.

When professional development opportunities are supported, they gather momentum as teachers think of more ways in which they can learn from each other and from experts in the field. The concrete ways you promote professional development show your staff how important this dimension is to your program.

The link is clear. One of the best predictors of a great place to work is the degree of emphasis placed on providing opportunities for staff to expand their knowledge base and improve their repertoire of skills. The more skilled teachers are, the more likely they are to experience, and be rewarded by, a high incidence of success. The more they experience success, the more likely they are to make a long-standing commitment to the center. Investing in professional development pays rich dividends to you program.

Supervise with a Focus on Reflection and Feedback

Do you know what factors contribute most to your teachers' sense of personal and professional fulfillment? Do you know the challenges they face with individual children in their care? Do you have a handle on the specific knowledge and skills that might help them feel more competent and capable in their roles? Are you familiar with their strengths? Getting teachers to reflect on the nitty-gritty of their work, the challenges they are experiencing, the areas where they feel most successful, and the ways they could feel more competent is at the heart of being a first-class supervisor.

There is no quick-fix strategy here that will work magic for your team. It's all about reflection and feedback, with an emphasis on a strengths-based approach. Central in the motivation equation is your ability to tailor your supervisory style to the developmental level of each teacher.

We take for granted the concept of developmental appropriateness when we think about our interactions with children, but we often forget that the same principle applies to adult supervisory and mentor relationships. Supervisory practices should vary depending on the teacher's career stage, degree of professional competence, and level of commitment. For some teachers this might entail a very directive approach. For others it will mean a collaborative or nondirective approach.

Management guru Peter Drucker reminds us that people are not machines. Machines can be worked, but humans must be developed. This distinction is critical to educational programs because of its implication for the way directors tap into the intrinsic motivation of staff. An integral part of the director's leadership role is helping teachers build opportunities for enrichment and personal achievement. Here are some questions you can ask teachers to help them become reflective practitioners and take ownership of their job satisfaction and professional growth.

- What is the most fulfilling part of your job?

- What talents, skills, special competencies, and unique contributions do you bring to the classroom?

- Do you have the opportunity every day to do what you do best?

- What keeps you from being as effective as you would like to be in your position?

- What resources do you need to excel in your job?

- If you had the power to change anything about your job, what would you change? Why would this be an improvement over existing conditions?

- What suggestions do you have for improving schedules, routines, and procedures so staff can function as a more effective team?

- If you could target one area of knowledge and skill building that would help you feel more competent and capable in your work, what would it be?

You may want to schedule a joint planning conference with each teacher twice a year to go over these questions. The purpose is to work together to chart each teacher's individual professional goals and to provide more focused feedback on performance. These one-on-one conferences breathe life into a job description and enable you as supervisor to facilitate each teacher's professional growth.

Think about these joint planning conferences as an opportunity to stimulate new ideas that might expand or enrich teachers' present jobs. That might mean adjusting assigned responsibilities to increase the scope of their work, visibility, or autonomy. The hope is that such adjustments will provide increased opportunities to experience achievement, recognition, advancement, and mastery in their day-to-day work. Enriching jobs can be a powerful stimulus to increase teachers' self-motivation.

Too often we underestimate the power of a touch, a smile, a kind word, a listening ear, an honest compliment, or the smallest act of caring, all of which have the potential to turn a life around.

Leo Buscaglia

All of us need to know we are valued for our hard work. When you give your staff open, honest, and regular feedback, you lay the foundation for respect and help develop feelings of self-worth. Feedback that is specific and shared in a supportive way can inspire staff and improve performance. The goal should be to help teachers reflect and analyze their actions and to begin to formulate their own strategies for improving their competence.

Teachers may also need intervention with specific feedback to help them resolve a nettlesome problem and get back on track. It is difficult to share authentic feedback and support if you have not spent any real time observing teachers working with children, so schedule regular times during the year to observe each teacher in action.

Seize the opportunity to make classroom observations a genuine partnership. Let your teachers take the lead in determining what they would like you to focus on. If they see your observation as supportive (as opposed to evaluative), they are less likely to be defensive and more likely to be open to your feedback and reflect on and improve their practice. Here is an example of one teacher's observation request.

Emma's Observation Request

Name: Emma Jones

I'd like to be observed on . . . Tuesday, October 3

I'd like to be observed during . . . Circle Time

Please look at . . . the children who are easily distracted. How can I help these kids stay focused during our circle time?

I need help with . . . knowing how to keep everyone in the group engaged and when it is appropriate to let a child go off and do another activity. I'm afraid if I lose one, I'll lose them all.

Capture anecdotes about things teachers do well along with areas for potential growth. When you provide feedback, here are some important things to keep in mind:

- Build on each person's strengths, focusing on unique interests, passions, and internal motivation.

- Concentrate on the teacher's behavior rather than on personality traits or general dispositions.

- Make your feedback specific rather than global.

- Provide feedback in a timely manner, the sooner after the observation, the better.

- Focus on the future rather than dwelling on the past.

- Decide on a feedback loop to check back and report on progress made.

It goes without saying that feedback needs to be ongoing, not just at annual performance reviews. Regular, open communication helps staff grow personally and professionally. Feedback is the mortar that cements professional relationships in any early childhood program. If teachers' jobs are structured to maximize intrinsic fulfillment, then you will have made an important stride in increasing individual job satisfaction and organizational commitment.

Strive for Clarity in Policies and Procedures

In many early childhood settings, jobs have a way of mushrooming out of control, with task after task piling up in an already ambiguous job description. Ill-defined job responsibilities are frustrating and stressful. Confusion and conflict result because there is lack of clarity about who is supposed to do what. Before you know it, you've got a storm brewing.

Teachers and assistants often work together as a team and share a range of responsibilities. In many programs, job titles, salaries, and educational levels do not distinguish the type of work a staff member does, although the amount of time spent on a task might vary between assistants, teachers, lead teachers, and even directors. There are always spills to be wiped up, activities to be prepared, field trips to be arranged, and parent meetings to be planned.

Often the job description is glanced at briefly at the time of hire and then filed away and forgotten about during the day-to-day functioning of a program. By default in many programs, the real description of roles and responsibilities are informally established by members of a teaching team. This can lead to conflict and strife if a classroom has a teacher with an assertive personality who decides that she wants to do the lion's share of curriculum planning, interacting with families, conducting assessments, and managing children's portfolios. If others on the team are left with mundane tasks and housekeeping chores, discontent and resentment will surely result.

The situation is different in other settings where all classroom staff are called *teacher* and treated as equals. This too offers challenges because less capable members of the team may implement inappropriate activities or talk to parents in an unprofessional manner. Differentiated roles where the most qualified teacher is designated as the lead teacher help ensure higher-level instructional practices and provide a career path for advancement for those with lower professional qualifications.

Directors need to periodically reexamine the structure of job designations so that job titles are based on skill and experience. The *Program Administration Scale* (PAS) can serve as a guide for differentiating roles. In addition, employees need to have a clear understanding of the limits of their work. They need to know not only what they are expected to do, but also what they are not expected to do.

One way to tap into teachers' perceptions about their role is to periodically distribute a role clarity questionnaire. The questionnaire asks about those aspects of a teacher's work that are well defined and going smoothly and those where greater clarity may be needed. Appendix D is an assessment tool from *Blueprint for Action*. Feel free to use it in your program. Directions for distributing the questionnaire and scoring instructions are included.

Beyond role expectations, center policies and procedures also need to be clearly articulated. Personnel policies pertaining to sick leave, absenteeism, maternity or paternity leave, grievance procedures, teacher preparation time, and expectations for teacher involvement in fundraising functions need to be put in writing and explained to new staff before they are hired.

Other general policies regarding sick children, first aid, administration of medicine, parent visits, transportation, field trips, fee payments, snacks and meals, and permission slips should also be put in writing to ensure that teachers understand what is expected of them. There are many excellent resources to guide directors in the writing of different center policies as they relate to these and other issues. Our favorites are *Developing and Administering a Child Care and Education Program* by Sciarra and Dorsey and *Planning and Administering Early Childhood Programs* by Decker, Decker, Freeman, and Knopf.

Take a moment now to think back to some of the questions that families and staff have asked you related to your center's policies and procedures. Did they ask the questions because they did not know where to find the information, or did they ask because the way the information was communicated verbally or written in the handbook was unclear or even confusing? If this is the case, think about ways you can reword or revise the policies so they are crystal clear and unambiguous.

Explore New Options for Rewards and Recognition

Wages, wages, wages! If you've been a director for more than ten minutes, you already know this is a major challenge in the early care and education field. Virtually every study examining early childhood teachers' job satisfaction indicates that practitioners are dissatisfied with the low pay and paltry benefits they receive. Teachers' salaries have never been high, but the situation seems to be worsening because salaries have not kept pace with inflation.

Demanding working conditions that include inadequate wages and meager benefits make it difficult to attract and retain good teachers, and program quality suffers as a result. Salaries and benefits are tied into the complex problem of how early childhood programs are funded. The problem is particularly acute in community-based programs that must compete with state-funded prekindergarten programs for the same pool of highly qualified teachers.

A 2008 study of the Illinois early childhood workforce, for example, found that lead teachers in community-based programs earned 44% less than their similarly qualified counterparts working in early childhood programs housed in public schools. The contrast in benefits was even more stark.

Salaries at the early childhood level will undoubtedly remain low for the foreseeable future. But that should not prevent directors from aggressively pursuing other avenues to promote a fair and equitable system of rewards. People work best when they know the philosophy underlying their pay and understand the potential for promotion. At a minimum, employees need to understand how decisions are made about salaries and promotions.

The key to a good compensation system is internal fairness (for example, an administrative assistant does not make more than a teacher) and external fairness (a teacher makes a comparable salary to teachers at other centers). Look again at the table on page 13 in Chapter 1 explaining internal and external equity.

Misunderstandings often occur when individuals do not have enough information on matters that directly affect their welfare. Many directors have been successful in eliminating the adversarial relationship between administration and staff by being more open about budgetary matters and sharing information regarding fiscal decisions. This need not be full disclosure about where every dollar is spent, but sometimes sharing with the staff concerns about the rising cost of insurance, the cost of workers' compensation, disability insurance, and the cost of utilities can give them a greater awareness of the complexities involved in balancing the budget.

The provision of breaks, vacation days, and sick days is certainly related to the adequacy of funds. But your attitude regarding staff benefits is critical. Emphasizing the value of teachers' taking regular breaks, spending time on vacation, and staying home when they are ill conveys to your staff that taking advantage of these policies does not mean lack of commitment to their jobs.

It is important, also, that substitute teacher policies do not put a burden on healthy staff. Money for paying substitutes must be budgeted, and teachers should be encouraged to use their sick days when they need to. Some centers have eliminated the term *sick days* altogether, replacing it with a more open policy of *mental health days*.

Many directors endorse a policy of differential pay based on merit. This conveys to teachers that they will be rewarded for performance and not just "putting in time." Merit increases can be tied to professional development and advanced degrees, as well as taking on additional responsibilities at the center.

Instituting merit pay plans can be tricky, though, as Daniel Pink, author of *Drive: The Surprising Truth about What Motivates Us*, points out. With any kind of extrinsic reward, expectations change and work that was once driven by intrinsic needs can be recast. Bottom line is, avoid rewards that are framed by "if/then."

Implementing a salary schedule and career ladder that ensures some degree of job security can also be a strong indicator to staff of your interest in their welfare. The appealing thing about career ladder plans is their potential for upgrading the professional orientation of staff. The research on career development of teachers indicates there are discernible stages in teachers' attainment of competencies that can be translated into natural ranks on a career ladder. A well thought-out career ladder recognizes and rewards good teaching performance and builds in incentives for job enrichment and expanded responsibilities.

Other centers have experimented with a variety of fringe benefit plans that are less expensive and easier to implement than increasing salaries across the board for all employees. These include free or reduced tuition for children of employees, reimbursement for courses taken for professional improvement, release time to visit other schools and attend conferences, access to the center's photocopy machine, free lunches, and paid membership fees to professional organizations.

Monetary rewards are not the only way you can convey respect for staff. Even after some solutions are found to help finance high-quality early care and education in this country, nonmonetary rewards will continue to be essential. Administrators know how important it is to respect teachers every day in even the smallest matters. The positive tone you set in your center will be picked up by parents and visitors from the community. You will also want to publicly recognize outstanding performance, perhaps through an annual awards program, a special display honoring a teacher's exceptional service, highlighting a staff accomplishment in the center's newsletter, or recognition at a parent/staff meeting.

As with if/then rewards, staff recognition programs can also be tricky. Try to avoid rewards that pit one employee against another. Rather, if you feel recognition is warranted, select individuals who have gone out of their way to support the whole team. Then you'll be reinforcing an organizational value of collegiality and helpfulness.

Sometimes it's the little things that make a difference. The following are some suggestions of different ways to recognize your staff. As you read the list, consider which type of recognition might be a good fit for each member of your team.

- Purchase a selection of gift cards that can be redeemed at a local merchant, restaurant, or bookstore. These might make worthy gifts to honor team members on their birthday or employment anniversary.

- Ask a veteran teacher to help orient a new employee. Explain in detail what qualifies the teacher for this important assignment.

- Reward teachers who have gone above and beyond by presenting them with a new children's book or flowering plant for their classroom.

- Schedule a masseuse for one of your monthly staff meetings to give neck and shoulder massages.

- Surprise your staff with a visit by a local ice cream vendor.

- Keep a stack of thank-you cards handy so you can write a personal note when a teacher does something extra to support a colleague.

- Kick off a staff meeting by inviting each team member to share a high point from the previous week.

- When teachers complete their degree or certificate, highlight their accomplishments in your center's newsletter and recognize them with a standing ovation at your staff meeting.

- Stock up on your teachers' favorite packaged snacks. Keep them in a basket in your office. When they stop by to talk about different issues, you can offer one.

- Periodically surprise a teacher with a certificate for a two-hour "long lunch" while you or a floater cover the classroom.

- Post teachers' photos and bios in your reception area.

- Order business cards for your teachers.

- Invite a teacher to accompany you to a community meeting or public event.

Finally, if you are concerned about the welfare of your teachers, you need to be proactive in advocating for higher wages and benefits. Provide parents with information about the full cost of quality, particularly how teachers' low salaries help make it possible for the center to have affordable tuition rates. Exercise 5 includes some additional things to consider.

What are you doing to advocate for improved wages and benefits for your staff?

☐ I post articles on the center's bulletin board about the importance of a highly trained workforce.

☐ I devote time to the topic of improved wages and benefits at parent meetings.

☐ I write at least one letter annually to my elective representatives about this issue.

☐ I vote for candidates who support early care and education.

☐ I participate on a public policy committee of a professional organization related to this issue.

☐ Our center's newsletter periodically includes information related to the cost of high-quality care.

☐ I write a letter to the editor of my local paper at least once a year about the importance of adequate compensation for early childhood professionals.

☐ I keep informed about new policy developments relating to early childhood workforce qualifications and compensation through updates from the Center for the Child Care Workforce (www.ccw.org).

Expand Teachers' Decision-Making Influence

You recognize that a quality early childhood classroom empowers children, offering them ample opportunity to make decisions about their play and learning experiences throughout the day. The same should be true when you set the stage for the adults working in your program. An integral part of a healthy climate is an uncompromising respect for people's need to have some say in the decisions that directly affect them. Whether the decision concerns curriculum, furniture arrangement, schedules for parent conferences, or field trip sites, teachers need to have input. When involvement is broadened, directors usually find that teachers feel a greater commitment to the program.

It is not easy to involve teachers and keep them informed. If you are not already including staff in decision making, you can gradually expand their participation by reviewing the range of decisions that are made and the consequences of those decisions. Look at the table "Types of Decisions" on pages 15–16 in Chapter 1, describing some of the many decisions made in early childhood programs. In most cases, these decisions fall into one of four categories:

A leader's power is finite, but a leader's shared power is infinite.

Lee Colan

- **Unilateral decision making.** Decisions that are best made by you alone.

- **Consultative decision making.** Decisions that are best made by you with input from your staff.

- **Collaborative decision making.** Decisions that can be made jointly by you and your staff.

- **Delegated decision making.** Decisions that should be made by the teachers or other staff exclusively.

Can you generate a list of unilateral decisions you've made this week? Now make a list of consultative or collaborative decisions made with teachers during the past week. Can you think of a delegated decision that teachers made recently? Directors sensitive to the importance of staff involvement will want to expand opportunities for teacher input through collaborative and delegated decision making. Deciding on the appropriate level varies according to the expertise, abilities, and interest of the parties involved.

Participatory management cannot be accomplished overnight. In many cases, behavior patterns and the dynamics of interpersonal relationships are well established, even firmly entrenched. Involvement cannot be thrust on people, but must be implemented gradually.

So how can you open channels for increased involvement without disrupting your program's continuity? First, you must actively and genuinely solicit feedback about how to improve working conditions. You can do it formally through climate assessment and informally as you talk with people every day.

Well-run and engaging staff meetings are another way to ensure that decision making increases. The number of meetings is not nearly as important as the kind of meetings and the degree to which agendas are jointly developed. Staff meetings can become the focal point for building team spirit and a cooperative management approach. When teachers feel comfortable enough to question procedures, suggest alternatives, and exchange different points of view, morale usually rises.

Take time now to complete Exercise 6. Review the listed items relating to areas in which teachers typically want more decision-making influence. Indicate those things you currently do, and those you may be able to implement in the near future.

Currently Doing	Planning to Implement	Areas for Involvement
☐	☐	**Interviewing and Hiring Staff** Teachers provide input in writing job announcements and job descriptions.
☐	☐	Teachers review candidate resumes and provide feedback and recommendations.
☐	☐	Teachers develop questions to ask interviewees.
☐	☐	Teachers participate in employee interviews.
☐	☐	**Determining Centerwide Goals and Objectives** Teachers review program objectives annually, making suggestions for refinements.
☐	☐	Teachers determine how program objectives are evident in the curriculum.
☐	☐	Teachers assist in developing staff meeting agendas.
☐	☐	**Training New Staff** Teachers help develop orientation policies and activities for new staff.
☐	☐	Teachers assist in training new employees.
☐	☐	Teachers serve as mentors for new employees.
☐	☐	**Parent and Community Relations** Teachers assist in determining types of parent education.
☐	☐	Teachers help develop parent newsletters.
☐	☐	Teachers help develop parent and community events.
☐	☐	**Planning Daily Activities** Teachers develop lesson plans as a classroom team.
☐	☐	Teachers determine daily schedules and classroom activities.
☐	☐	Teachers determine how to set up their classroom.
☐	☐	Teachers assist in determining field trips.
☐	☐	**Ordering Materials and Supplies** Teachers contribute ideas for needed materials and supplies.
☐	☐	Teachers are given a budget to spend on needed supplies.

Strengthen the Focus on Mission and Vision

The whirlwind pace of most early childhood directors leaves precious little time to stand back and contemplate the bigger picture of their center's mission and vision. But a central part of your role as leader is to help crystallize your center's mission and develop a shared vision among your staff and board. Organizational mission and vision statements that reflect the collective values within the center help create a unity of purpose and serve as the foundation for goal setting. A mission statement focuses on the purpose of your program. A vision statement is a mental picture of what you hope to accomplish.

No doubt about it, constructing mission and vision statements that reflect the collective beliefs and values of all involved takes time and patience. Directors who value the process of collaboration with staff are generally more willing to devote the necessary time to involve staff in exploring shared values and setting goals for their program. They know that the very process of engaging staff in exploring core values, beliefs, and assumptions results in staff having a deeper connection and commitment to the program.

This kind of work should not be hurried; it should span several months. You can start the process with a brainstorming session at a staff meeting. Simply ask folks to create their own separate list of words or phrases that describe the values most important to them in an early care and education program. They should come up with five to ten words pretty quickly. Then, in round-robin fashion, ask each teacher to share one idea as you record them on flip-chart paper. Continue going around until all their words are posted. Finally, facilitate a discussion about the list, commenting on words and phrases that were mentioned more than once.

Continue exploring values and beliefs with additional questions, recording statements on flip-chart paper so there is always a visual record of all contributions:

- What do we stand for?

- How do we (and how should we) define success in our work?

- How do we want to be known in the community?

- What traits and outcomes do we want children to reflect as a result of their experience at the center?

The next step is to explore how your agreed-on organizational values are reflected in practice. Here are some questions to guide that exploration:

- How do our interactions with children and parents provide concrete evidence of our core values?

- How does our center's descriptive literature and current mission statement reflect our core values? Is anything missing? Should any wording be revised?

- How does the physical environment reflect our core values?

- How does the curriculum reflect our core values?

- Are the processes of our program—the way decisions are made, how meetings are conducted, how information is communicated to families— reflective of our core values?

By this stage, you and your team will have a pretty good handle on what you need to do to update your center's mission and vision statements.

In their inspiring book *The Visionary Director*, Margie Carter and Deb Curtis provide many more ideas and suggestions on how to work with your team to craft a shared vision for your center. As you engage in this important work, it is vital that each person on your staff feels like his or her voice is heard and contributions valued.

Your mission and vision statements provide the foundation on which your annual goals and educational objectives are developed. Whatever method you use to achieve consensus on the goals and objectives, it is important that they be realistic and that progress in achieving them can be measured in concrete ways.

Having a clear set of educational goals and objectives that your team agrees on ensures that teachers' efforts will be in line with the broader mission of your organization. Well-formulated goals also help teachers set priorities when making decisions about appropriate curriculum experiences for young children. Finally, consensus on goals can reduce teacher anxiety because it provides staff with a kind of benchmark by which to measure progress.

Author Rick DuFour couldn't agree more. He states, "Schools stumble when their leaders cannot identify priorities, or when they seem to say, 'Pay attention to everything; everything is important.' Schools will never have a widely shared sense of purpose and priorities until their leaders can help the educators within them cut through the noise and clarify 'this is what is important, this is what we stand for, this is what we strive toward.'"

When you discover your mission, you will feel its demand. It will fill you with enthusiasm and a burning desire to get to work on it.

W. Clement Stone

Every director is confronted with urgent business every day, so it is easy to find a myriad of good excuses to put off values clarification, vision building, and the goal-setting process for another year. But making time for this collaborative process will pay rich dividends in strengthening staff relations and achieving a unified sense of purpose among your team. As your group's divergent viewpoints are merged into a unified harmonious whole, this self-renewing process will help you and your teachers strengthen your professional partnership.

Manage and Protect Time

Just how do you create the right balance between professional efficiency and warm informality, between seriousness and silliness, between paperwork and people work, between process and product? To be sure, educating young children is not like building weather vanes; worker productivity cannot be gauged in discrete units, like the notches on a thermometer. But we can use our time wisely to ensure the center runs efficiently and effectively and minimizes job-related stress.

Employing a host of time management strategies is one way to begin using time more wisely. For example, one strategy is to do similar tasks—writing letters, sending e-mails, filing papers, making phone calls, or running errands—at the same time. Grouping activities allows you to focus your attention and make your day less fragmented.

Your ability to set priorities, target time, and avoid procrastination certainly has a beneficial impact on your staff's ability to perform their jobs well. Your efficient and effective use of time also serves as a powerful role model for others, particularly for new staff, who may be struggling to balance the demands of their personal and professional lives.

Workloads consist of both the sheer quantity of tasks to be accomplished and the time frame in which those jobs must be done. Too much to do in too little time (work overload) or too little to do that is stimulating (boredom) are both sources of job stress and can result in lower job satisfaction and performance.

Because people differ in background and training, the trick for administrators is to find the right balance for each person—matching individuals to specific jobs so that they feel challenged and stretched yet not overwhelmed and consumed by too much work pressure. Holding individual conferences periodically to review each teacher's workload, needs, interests, and competencies can demonstrate your interest in their welfare.

There is another way directors can communicate genuine concern for their teachers: help them understand the emotional limits of their work. If they are losing sleep worrying about a particular child or putting in too much time preparing activities for their classroom, help them understand that being dedicated and loyal to an organization and a mission does not mean that they must be consumed by their professional obligations. *Dedication does not mean deadication!*

Indeed, as role models, directors can help employees understand that survival in a field that demands so much psychic energy depends on the ability to lead a balanced life and look after our own mental health. A certain amount of detachment from one's professional role may be essential in maintaining a healthy perspective. Learning how to emotionally leave one's job at the end of the day is one important way to achieve that. Here are some other ways to balance workloads:

- Have a system in place to ensure that teachers have adequate breaks from the classroom.

- Establish a policy that allows staff to leave the building during their lunch break.

- Build in time during staff meetings for quiet reflection.

- Ensure that the substitute pool is adequate or hire a floater teacher so that teachers can take vacation and sick days without feeling guilty.

- Encourage staff to take a walk outside during breaks.

Another strategy to help your teachers realistically evaluate their workload and make adjustments as necessary is to review their job descriptions and group their responsibilities into four or five categories. Then have them assign a percentage to the time they spend in each category over the course of a week. The percentages should total 100%. Here is an example of an analysis completed by a teacher.

Activity or Task	% of time
Interactions with children	70%
• Greeting children at arrival	
• Supervising children's free play	
• Leading group time	
• Managing daily routines—breakfast, lunch, nap, toileting	
• Collecting documentation for children's portfolios	
• Conducting observations and assessments	
• Assembling children's belongings for dismissal	
Lesson planning	10%
• Attending team meetings	
• Preparing for activities	
• Writing lessons	
Family partnerships	5%
• Connecting with parents at arrival and dismissal	
• Writing a classroom newsletter	
• Connecting with parents by phone and e-mail	
• Planning and attending parent meetings	
• Attending parent conferences	
Physical environment	10%
• Arranging the classroom	
• Setting up activities	
• Cleaning up activities and organizing materials	
Miscellaneous	5%
• Attending centerwide meetings	
• Attending professional development workshops	
• Mentoring other staff	
• Preparing performance appraisal materials	

Jessica's Workload Analysis

Once the analyses are completed, ask the teachers to describe the categories they came up with and how they arrived at the percentages they assigned to each.

- Do the percentages seem realistic?

- Does it seem like they focus too much time on some tasks that are not as important as others? Do they need to shift the times they are spending on certain responsibilities?

- Can they realistically achieve their responsibilities in the time they have?

- Can any responsibilities be reassigned to someone else, or even dropped?

Open and direct conversations about workload can be the springboard for developing more efficient and effective practices that will improve center operations.

Address Adult Needs in the Physical Environment

Most early childhood environments are designed primarily with the needs of young children in mind. But accommodating your staff's needs is an important issue in assuring a healthy professional work environment. A poorly equipped or hastily designed environment can promote tension and frustration or even result in physical injury.

The spatial layout of a center conveys strong nonverbal messages that affect employees' perceptions and overall morale. For example, a teacher preparation room sends a strong message about the value of teacher planning. Likewise, sufficient space to park, a place for personal belongings, and a place to escape during the day for a few minutes of solitude all symbolize how much teachers are valued and respected.

Issues concerning the use of space in early childhood programs are particularly important because shared space is the rule of thumb in most centers. Directors who understand the impact of the physical setting on worker morale will find creative ways to make the use of space conducive to achieving their program goals. Here are some questions to consider:

- Does the spatial arrangement allow the center's administrative work to be conducted without interfering with the children's activities?

- Do teachers have a quiet place to hold a parent conference or have a personal telephone conversation?

- Is there sufficient space to store classroom equipment and ample work surfaces to prepare class materials?

- Do all classrooms have comfortable places for adults to sit and be with children?

- Are teachers encouraged to add artifacts, photographs, and other objects to their classrooms that reflect their lives and the lives of the children in their care?

- Do employees have a safe, secure place to put personal belongings?

- Is your staff room fully equipped with educational supplies (laminating machine, paper cutter, duplicating machine), comfortable adult furnishings, computers, and access to the Internet?

- Is there is a professional library where teachers can find books and journals and check out DVDs dealing with early childhood topics?

- Is the physical setting as it relates to the health and safety needs of employees evaluated periodically?

- Is the overall maintenance of the facility the responsibility of someone other than teachers?

Poor arrangement of space can cause a host of potential health and safety hazards. Poor lighting, improper ventilation, and high noise levels can make it difficult for teachers to carry out their responsibilities. Programs where more than one classroom share the same open space need to be mindful of adequate sound-absorbing materials or establish other mechanisms to reduce the noise from surrounding rooms.

Still, accommodating adult needs in a child-size environment is not easy. Low counters, small chairs, and child-size fixtures are essential elements in good programs for young children, but may contribute to stress and physical fatigue for the adults who must maneuver in these settings. Select and arrange furniture and fixtures to minimize the incidence of injury, health hazards, and lower back strain. And be sure to check that building materials, insulation, drapes, or carpets do not emit harmful toxins.

You and your staff can work closely to evaluate the work environment, make changes, and then review how successful those changes are. Take photos to give yourselves a fresh perspective about the use of space. Visit other centers to see what works well.

If your center has a staff lounge, take a few minutes to go there and find a comfortable spot to sit. Look around the room and reflect as you complete Exercise 7. Making improvements in the staff lounge might be a good first step toward improving the physical environment.

Assessing the Staff Lounge	Yes	No
There is a staff bulletin board.	☐	☐
There is a space for teachers to share ideas and resources.	☐	☐
There are announcements of professional development opportunities.	☐	☐
There are professional journals and magazines available.	☐	☐
There are comfortable places to sit and relax.	☐	☐
There are inspirational quotes posted.	☐	☐
There are photos of teachers at work with children and one another.	☐	☐
There are ways for staff to learn about each other's lives.	☐	☐
There is evidence showing that supervisors care about staff—notes of encouragement, kudos for achievements, expressions of support.	☐	☐
There is a place to provide suggestions for center improvements.	☐	☐
There is a place for teachers to show support for one another—notes of appreciation, pictures, poems, phrases of support.	☐	☐
Humorous cartoons and jokes are posted. Playful props are available to encourage laughter and balance.	☐	☐
There is a place for staff to store and prepare their food for lunch and breaks.	☐	☐
A laminating machine, paper cutter, photocopier, and other equipment and resources are available.	☐	☐
Teachers have access to the Internet.	☐	☐
There are things to nurture and pamper staff—natural light, plants, flowers, pillows, blankets, soft music, pleasant aromas, healthy snacks.	☐	☐

For the items you indicated *no*, are these possibilities available elsewhere in the center?

Increase Opportunities for Creativity and Innovation

Don't let limited resources hold you and your staff back from pursuing great ideas! It's important to recognize that creativity and innovation are not the same thing. Creativity focuses on the sharing of ideas, and innovation is the vehicle whereby creative ideas are implemented. The good news is that innovation can be fostered by people who are not particularly creative, assuming they can recognize creativity in others and provide the work climate in which it can thrive.

The only way to unleash the creative energy in an organization is to encourage staff to try new techniques and instructional approaches. Whether teachers are interested in implementing a new curriculum, experimenting with cutting-edge technology, or exploring different ways to engage families as educational partners, their efforts need to be supported. Find ways to allow those imaginations to soar!

Encouragement and support, however, should not be limited to praising successes. Teachers also need to know that occasional setbacks are understood to be part of the innovation process. Innovation is directly linked with change. And in any area of organizational change, the director's attitude is most important. If you approach change with enthusiasm and confidence, that spirit will be conveyed to your team. Your role as leader is to pave the way for change, keep channels of communication open, and provide support as needed.

Openness to change is not a trait that can be readily measured during the selection of new staff, but it is a trait that can be nurtured in the right supportive atmosphere. Taking time to consider the reasons for a teacher's resistance to an organizational change is the first step toward creating an environment that respects different degrees of openness to new ideas.

Resistance is often based on fear of the unknown. Such anxiety can be alleviated by involving staff as much as possible in the planning and implementation of decisions, keeping them well informed, and providing as much time as possible to allow reluctant staff members to psychologically gear up for impending changes.

Divergent thinking and creativity can also be nurtured by helping staff develop new strategies for looking at old problems. Devoting one meeting each month to brainstorming solutions to centerwide problems is one way to unleash creativity, generate new ideas, and share multiple perspectives.

In organizations where everyone thinks alike, no one thinks very much.

Walter Lippmann

Another way to encourage innovation is to ask questions that encourage people to think outside of the box. Even when you think they've solved a problem or come up with a great plan, don't rush to closure. Take a few minutes to keep the creative juices flowing by asking the following questions:

- Can anything else be added to this idea to achieve an even better outcome?

- Could we take anything away from this idea to make it more streamlined yet still effective?

- Is there any minor tweaking that needs to be done before we implement the idea?

- Could there be an even more effective way to achieve our purpose that we haven't thought of yet?

There is no shortage of playful books on the market filled with interesting games, puzzles, tips, and brainteasers for breaking through mental blocks and tapping creative potential. Selecting one of the many exercises or games presented in these books to use at the beginning of each staff meeting will not only be an interesting warm-up, but will help get your teachers working together in new, creative ways. Two of our favorites are *Conceptual Blockbusting*, by James Adams, and *Thinkertoys: A Handbook of Creative-Thinking Techniques*, by Michael Michalko. One of these books might also make an ideal present for your teachers.

Finally, make sure there is a suggestion box or a "Bright Ideas" bulletin board somewhere in the center that invites staff to submit serious and silly entries. You can even create fun recognition prizes for folks who dream up creative ways to save the center some money or achieve greater efficiency.

You can't be creative unless you agree to be confused.

Margaret Wheatley

CHAPTER 6

Clear Skies Ahead—From Assessment to Action

As a leader, you play a pivotal role in both assessing current work attitudes and structuring changes to improve conditions. As you consider a plan for assessing your program, keep in mind that this kind of leadership does not just happen. You must carve out a leadership role that makes healthy work life issues a central priority. More than any other individual, you are the change agent that can have the greatest impact on the program's organizational climate.

In this chapter, you'll hear the stories of how four directors took steps to improve the organizational climate of their programs. They each took a unique path based on data they collected about their programs. Maria did a formal organizational climate assessment to confirm her gut feelings about the area she needed to focus on in her program improvement efforts. Sandra, Carmen, and Jon based their action plans on data gathered from shorter, more informal surveys. These case studies provide some vivid examples of how you can move your program by structuring changes to improve work life conditions.

Maria Increases Teachers' Decision-Making Influence

Maria is the new director of a large nonprofit child care center. She was just promoted to the position from her lead teacher role when Patricia, the director for 12 years, left to accept a new job in another state. The first day in her new role, Maria walked into the staff lounge during the busy lunch hour and the room fell silent. No one said a word to her or made eye contact. Maria walked back into her office, closed the door and sobbed. Just the week before those same teachers were her peers. Now, with her new title, everything seemed different.

The odd thing was that Maria wasn't even certain she wanted this job. Patricia had played the part of a "mother hen" taking care of everything and making all the decisions for the program. Maria was too young to take on the role of anyone's mother. In taking on this position, one thing she wanted to do differently was consider how decisions were made.

Maria knew from her own experience how powerless it felt to be a teacher at the center. In the past, Patricia had been responsible for purchasing educational materials and determining the curriculum and lesson plans; she even rearranged classroom furniture if she didn't like the way a room was set up.

Occasionally Patricia sought input from the staff, but it always turned out to be an artificial overture. Like the time Patricia asked the teachers if they thought scheduling Back-to-School Night for 5:00 p.m. was a good idea. The teachers unanimously said that five o'clock was a difficult time to host this kind of school event for children, parents, and themselves. The debate went round and round. Finally, Patricia pulled out a stack of flyers she had already printed announcing Back-to-School Night at 5:00 p.m. Why waste teachers' valuable time if she'd already made the decision?

Maria's sense that others also felt the decision-making structure of the center needed to be changed was confirmed when she looked at the results of the Work Environment Profile the center had just received. Prior to Patricia's departure, the staff had completed the *Early Childhood Work Environment Survey*. Looking at the dimension of decision making in Part A of the profile, Maria noted the score was only 3.5 out of 10, indicating that staff felt the director held tight control over most center decisions. In Part B of the profile, 18 out of 21 staff had indicated that "involvement in decision making" was one of three aspects of their work that was most important to them. And in Part F of the profile, there was a huge discrepancy between teachers' current decision-making influence and their desired level of decision-making influence in the five areas described.

Maria felt that if she could make some simple changes to involve teachers in making decisions for the program, she might be able to turn the cold-shoulder treatment she had experienced into a more collaborative team spirit. The first part of this process was to educate the staff on the possible levels of participation in decision making. Maria made copies of "Levels of Participation" from the book *Circle of Influence* to share and discuss at a staff meeting.

The second part of her plan was to become more intentional in the distribution of decision-making influence. Each time a major decision needed to be made about the program, Maria would share with staff her rationale for taking a unilateral, consultative, collaborative, or delegated approach. This way the teachers would have a clear understanding of their level of participation in a given decision. When the governing board made a decision about salary increases, Maria took the time to explain to her team the rationale for their unilateral decision.

The final part of Maria's new plan to expand decision-making influence was to take another quick assessment. She completed the exercise that is found on page 71. The results, along with informal discussions with staff, led Maria to establish new procedures. Here are three examples of levels of staff participation and the positive actions and spirit they engendered:

- **Consultative decision making.** Maria allotted each classroom a quarterly budget to purchase new educational materials. The teachers were delighted to have the opportunity to have input on selecting their own materials. They submitted their proposal to Maria for approval, which led to a conversation about what their plans were for the new materials. Not only did this process empower the teachers, it gave Maria a way to keep engaged in what was happening in the classrooms.

- **Collaborative decision making.** Maria posted a staff meeting agenda on the bulletin board in the staff lounge a week before each scheduled staff meeting. She invited teachers to add topics for inclusion in the agenda. This helped move staff meetings from being just a laundry list of director announcements to including more interactive conversations about topics of high interest to the teachers.

- **Delegated decision making.** Maria provided examples of how other child care centers celebrated the Week of the Young Child. She asked if any volunteers would like to take the lead in creating a Week of the Young Child event for the center. The staff formed a committee of teachers and was given a small budget. They worked tirelessly for a month to plan a children's festival, complete with food, games, an auction of children's artwork, and pony rides. The children's festival ended up becoming a beloved annual event of the program.

Maria's strategy clearly worked. Within six months of assuming the directorship, she felt genuine acceptance by and respect from the staff. The teachers grew to appreciate having someone who had walked in their shoes holding this leadership role. Maria continued to find new ways to involve teachers in decision making. Over time, the workplace seemed to come alive; people were more engaged. Teachers expressed a sense of pride and ownership over the welfare of the program. As Maria walked past the staff lounge one day she overheard teachers brainstorming ways to get the playground renovated. Clearly they were feeling part of the decision making process!

Sandra Encourages Greater Collegiality

Sandra is the director of a for-profit child care program that is part of a national chain. The center had recently experienced a lot of changes and staff turnover. In fact, Sandra was the sixth director in the past three years. She was undaunted by the center's reputation as a revolving door for early childhood teachers. In fact, she was eager to take on the challenge. She had engineered a turnaround in morale at her previous program and felt confident she could achieve the same outcome here, even though circumstances were somewhat different.

Pretty quickly Sandra realized what she was up against. Staff relations were frosty, to say the least. There seemed to be an ever-present tension in even the smallest interactions between teachers. Most noticeable to Sandra was the absence of laughter in the center. The children were clearly affected by the heavy cloud of tension that hung over the center. The staff lounge looked like a deserted wasteland. Sandra was surprised to learn there had not been any centerwide staff meetings in over a year. And team meetings were frequently canceled due to shortages of teachers. Essentially, everyone was isolated in their own classroom.

Sandra was convinced there was a direct correlation between the high teacher turnover, the breakdown in communications, the overemphasis on autonomy, and the overall low morale. The center had no established methods for teachers to exchange information, share ideas, or support one another. Sandra's work was cut out for her, to be sure. But she was determined to improve the relationships among teachers, inspire enthusiasm for the important work they were doing, and build stronger commitment to the center's mission.

As Sandra reflected on strategies for moving forward, she thought it best to proceed cautiously. She realized that building trusting and cooperative working relationships would not happen overnight. She decided the first step was to make the staff lounge more inviting and welcoming.

Sandra completed the staff lounge assessment that was presented earlier on page 79. She shared the results with her regional manager, who agreed that the staff lounge space resembled the aftermath of a tornado. Without telling the staff, Sandra and the regional manager, along with Sandra's son, who was home from college, worked nonstop over a weekend to spruce up the space—a fresh coat of paint, a new bookcase, pictures, plants, and a cozy sofa and pillows purchased at a garage sale. Within 48 hours and at minimal expense, the staff lounge was transformed into an inviting oasis.

When Sandra's teachers arrived for work on Monday morning, they suspected something might be up when they saw their old coffee-stained carpet sitting in the dumpster. Needless to say, they were blown away by the work that Sandra and her covert team had put into renovating the lounge.

As Sandra had hoped, this act was the catalyst for changing the tone of co-worker interactions. Because everyone was eager to spend time in this beautiful new space, spontaneous acts of collegiality started to take place. Teachers brought in their own books and curriculum guides to put on the bookshelves for others to read. They posted inspirational quotes on the wall. The bulletin board became a showcase for photos of the staff's children, pets, and events that had occurred in their personal lives.

Sandra was pleased, but she knew there was still more to do before she achieved her goal of establishing a true team. Her next step was even more ambitious. She developed an action plan that focused on improving communication systems and promoting greater collegiality.

Action Steps	Resources Needed
Establish monthly centerwide staff meetings	• adjustment of administrators' and teachers' work hours for meeting days • budget adjustment to cover overtime pay for six teachers • multipurpose room reserved for evening meeting
Create an end-of-the-year staff retreat	• $800 allocated from parent committee fundraising campaign • release time provided for retreat committee to plan activities
Create a "Bright Ideas" bulletin board	• $10 gift cards awarded at staff meetings for creative Bright Ideas posted each month (voted on by staff)

At the first centerwide staff meeting, Sandra shared a new goal: launching more opportunities for staff to work together on projects and support one another in their work. She used the "I Value a Co-Worker Who Is..." handout as a warm-up activity (Appendix C). She asked each person to share what they valued most in a co-worker. Through this discussion the group discovered that the trait checked by everyone was *collaborative*. They decided to brainstorm a list of new ways they might work collaboratively. This list included:

- Each classroom teaching team will serve as host for a centerwide staff meeting. The host team will devote the first ten minutes of the meeting to sharing a classroom success story or new curriculum idea that worked for their group. They will also bring a snack to share.

- Create an "article club" that meets monthly for a potluck dinner. Each month the club will discuss an article from *Young Children* that was relevant to their work.

- Design a system for teachers to observe each other's classrooms once a month for an hour.

- Form a committee to create an end-of-the-year picnic for families and staff.

- Create a committee to plan a weekend staff retreat.

Sandra was ecstatic about the outcomes she achieved in a relatively short period of time. She knew it was critical to follow through and make sure these new ideas for collaboration came to fruition. She generated a list of tasks, timelines, and people responsible for each of the new ideas. She worked to ensure adequate coverage so the various committees would have time to meet and that teachers could observe each other's classrooms. Sandra tried not to become overly optimistic about these changes, but she felt confident that a transformation was taking place—her *group* of teachers was becoming a *team* of teachers.

Gradually the dark cloud that seemed to be hovering over Sandra's center started to dissipate. Teachers began visiting one another's classrooms and supporting each other on different child management issues. There was humor and spontaneous laughter.

One hot summer day, Sandra happened into the staff lounge. A group of teachers from different classrooms were enjoying their break together. They had pulled a small wading pool into the staff lounge and filled it with cold water. The teachers were all gathered around the pool, splashing their bare feet in the water. They burst into laughter when Sandra smiled and said, "What creative problem solving on such a hot day!" Little did they know she was filled with joy in witnessing this expression of camaraderie.

Carmen Expands Opportunities for Professional Growth

Carmen has been the director of a private for-profit program in a large urban area for 12 years. Her program is one of three centers owned by a business-savvy young couple. Once they were confident in Carmen's leadership abilities, the couple pretty much maintained a hands-off policy, allowing her the freedom to hire staff and run the center as she saw fit.

One of the teachers in Carmen's center is Laura. Laura has been a preschool teacher for nearly 19 years. Each year she implements the same curriculum themes—dinosaurs in the fall, community helpers in the winter, farm animals in the spring, and ocean life in the summer. Laura finds comfort in the predictability of this curriculum. She knows them like the back of her hand and her lesson plans require little preparation since she has been using the same themes for almost two decades.

Meanwhile, in the classroom next door, life is a bit more unpredictable; some might say it is teetering on the chaotic. Claire is an energetic new teacher. She recently earned her associate's degree in early childhood and is now in her second year of teaching. Claire believes the day should be unstructured, allowing ample opportunity for free play. Unfortunately, some of the parents are becoming concerned that "no real learning" is taking place in the midst of what appears to be mayhem.

While Carmen has always supported a variety of professional development options for her teachers, she has done little to ensure follow through or a consistent approach across classrooms. Recently, however, she read about a constructivist approach to learning and the importance of job-embedded professional development. She has been thinking about her own experiences working in a campus lab school where a great deal of time was dedicated to inquiry and reflection. She had loved that approach when she was a graduate student and wondered why she hadn't fostered a culture of inquiry in her own center. Carmen wanted her teachers to have a similar opportunity.

Carmen decided to implement a bold new approach to professional development at her center. She knew, though, that she needed to carefully pave the way for such change. Her first step was to share some articles with her teachers that described how other programs had launched professional learning communities. At a staff meeting, she asked the teachers to consider what a learning community might look like at their center and what they would need to get started. There was clearly some skepticism, as evidenced by the blank faces. For example, Laura spent most of the meeting with her arms folded and her head down, choosing not to participate in the discussion.

Carmen decided to bring in Arianna, an educational consultant, to help her implement a learning community. Arianna was highly respected in the field and her workshops were always well attended by both new and experienced teachers. Arianna suggested that Carmen introduce the project approach to the staff as a springboard for building a culture of inquiry. Knowing that the focus of the project approach was to get children to investigate things they were interested in, Carmen agreed that it might set the stage for the teachers to become researchers themselves. She felt the approach was appropriate also because it would honor the teachers' desire to organize the curriculum in their own classrooms while still maintaining a consistent philosophical approach across classrooms.

Arianna took on the role of facilitator for the curriculum study group meetings. While there was some hesitation when the idea of the project approach was first introduced, those issues quickly disappeared. The teachers were pleased at how readily the children focused on their class projects. Laura's class decided they wanted to learn more about where all their trash went, and Claire's class had lots of questions about water. With Arianna's guidance and support, the teachers quickly mastered the steps of the project approach.

At each study group meeting, Arianna offered probing questions for the teachers to consider:

- What were the children most interested in learning about?

- What would you change in the classroom to expand children's learning?

- What do you wish you could explore more deeply?

- How could we include the families in this experience?

- What skills are the children learning through their explorations?

As the months passed, the focus on inquiry and children's learning became the norm at the center. Teachers devoted significant time exploring how to deepen and enrich children's interests. Families became active participants in both sharing their knowledge and bringing in materials to enhance the class projects. The classrooms were filled with rich documentation about all the discoveries being made. Systematic investigation and problem solving were woven into all aspects of classroom life. There was a greater focus on observation and wonder.

Laura surprised herself by finding it easy to give up the tried-and-true seasonal themes she had depended on for so many years. The project approach rejuvenated her enthusiasm for teaching. She announced at one of the curriculum study group meetings that she never wanted to do another unit on dinosaurs again! This new method succeeded by tapping into children's interests and their learning was far richer. For Claire, the project approach gave a focus to the classroom and helped her to structure children's learning while still allowing ample opportunity for play and exploration.

The most surprising outcome, from Carmen's perspective, was that Laura and Claire became partners in supporting each other, overcoming obvious differences in age and teaching style. They would jot down notes about something that happened in the classroom and ponder together what it might mean and how to broaden the experience. Carmen was proud at what she had accomplished at the center for the children and for the teachers.

Jon Takes Steps to Improve Supervisory Support

Jon is the site director of a Head Start program that is part of a large social service agency. He oversees eight teachers, eight assistant teachers, and a parent support coordinator. Over the six years he has been with this center, he has experienced the typical ebb and flow of funding problems so characteristic of nonprofits. He has also experienced the seismic tremors that spread throughout the Head Start community every time the government mandates new Head Start standards or program requirements. Jon has to admit, though, that the requirement of increasing Head Start staff qualifications forced him to examine his own center's approach to supervision and professional development.

Jon decided he needed some data in order to decide how to proceed. He distributed the short version of the *Early Childhood Work Environment Survey* to his entire staff. He took a deep breath when he got the tabulated results. While his teachers gave a fairly high rating to the item "Supervisors are knowledgeable and competent," the lowest rating on the survey was for the item "Supervisors provide helpful feedback." The next lowest rating was for the item "Staff are encouraged to learn new skills and competencies." There was no hiding from it. Since he was the only person in a supervisory role, these ratings were obviously about him.

At the next staff meeting, Jon decided to face the issue directly. He stated that he had always prided himself on giving teachers autonomy and lots of latitude to do as they wanted to in their classrooms. Now he realized that his hands-off approach was not good. He promised that he would begin working with them one-on-one to provide more focused support and feedback.

Using the resources in the book *Blueprint for Action,* Jon decided to implement an individualized model of supervision and staff development. He felt that if he could tap into the individual needs, expectations, and motivations of each of the teachers, he could help them improve their professional competence and perhaps even motivate them to take additional formal coursework to increase their qualifications.

Jon began by meeting with teachers individually to talk about their roles and responsibilities. In preparation for these meetings, he had each teacher complete the Role Perceptions Questionnaire (Appendix D). This served as a great springboard for their first discussion. He was surprised at how hungry his teachers were for this kind of dialogue. Not one of his meetings was completed in the half hour he had allotted. Several took a good 90 minutes or more.

The next step was to schedule monthly observations in each classroom. In the past Jon was uncomfortable in the role of observer, which is why he seldom did it. This time he decided to take a different approach, asking teachers to tell him one thing they wanted him to focus on—a particular child, the way the classroom was set up, or an activity the teacher had planned.

By making these observation times a teacher-supervisor partnership, Jon's entire attitude about providing feedback changed. Now, he relished the opportunity to meet with his teachers afterward, because he saw how much they respected his perspective and objective opinion and that their intentionality and interactions with children were improving as a result. It was also easier to give staff critical feedback in an area they expressed a need to improve on.

Ten months after he had done the initial ECWES survey, Jon decided to administer the survey again. He was elated by how much the teachers' perceptions of supervisory support had changed. In fact, teachers' perceptions of the overall climate also improved significantly. His focus on goal setting with his teachers, encouraging reflection, and providing specific feedback was clearly changing people's perceptions of the center as a workplace. While these changes were noteworthy, the most profound change occurred in Jon himself. His confidence in his ability to guide and support his teachers was elevated, and he found a renewed sense of purpose in his role as instructional leader.

CHAPTER 7

A Final Word

You have learned in this book that achieving a healthy quality of work life is both a goal and a process—it is what we work toward and the means by which we reach that goal. A good climate makes it possible to work effectively to meet the needs of young children and achieve program goals. It also makes the work environment a pleasant place to spend time.

You've also learned from the many vignettes and case studies included that the best programs are those where administrators, teachers, and support staff engage jointly in solving problems, making decisions, and implementing changes as needed. Although you play a key leadership role at your center, creating a great place to work is not your responsibility alone. The assessment process, the interpretation of results, and the implementation of a plan to strengthen the dimensions of organizational climate should be a collaborative process. This sends a strong message: We are all in this together.

Because we spend such a substantial portion of our lives at work, it is very important that work settings be structured to address both the head and the heart—to feed our intrinsic drive to master new skills and the need for meaningful work. All early childhood educators deserve to work in environments that use their talents and develop their professional capabilities. Andy Hargreaves said it best when he wrote, "What we want for our children we should want for their teachers; that schools be places of learning for both of them, and that such learning be suffused with excitement, engagement, passion, challenge, creativity, and joy."

We hope you are convinced that quality of work life isn't a peripheral issue. It is the essence of effective leadership. Directors of exemplary programs are like barometers—they constantly assess fluctuations in their organizational climate and they work to make adaptations as necessary. They use the information from formal and informal climate assessment not only to forecast, but also to shape the climate in which they and their staff work.

Sometimes in the winds of change we find our true direction.

Unknown

Addressing quality of work life issues needs to be an ongoing endeavor. Just as wind patterns and weather conditions are constantly changing, the context of your program and the challenges you face are constantly changing. That means there will always be new issues to deal with. After all, weather is never constant, and sometimes a good forecast turns bad. This book has provided you with a variety of assessment tools and valuable strategies to get started in making your center a great place to work. The ten dimensions of organizational climate should serve as a convenient framework to guide your quality of work life improvement efforts and benchmark your progress.

I slept and dreamt that life was joy. I awoke and found that life was duty. I went to work and discovered that duty can be joy.

—Tagore, Bengali Poet

For Further Reading

Adams, J. L. (2001). *Conceptual Blockbusting*. New York, NY: Basic Books.

Albrecht, K. (2002). *The Right Fit: Recruiting, selecting, and orienting staff*. Lake Forest, IL: New Horizons.

Albrecht, K., & Engel, B. (2007, July). Moving away from a quick-fix mentality to systematic professional development. *Young Children, 62*(4), 18–25.

Barth, R. (2006, March). Improving relationships within the schoolhouse. *Educational Leadership*, 8–13.

Battersby, M. E. (2005, January/February). Find, attract, and retain workers with affordable benefits. *Exchange*, 14–18.

Bella, J. (2008, July/August). Improving leadership and management practices one step at a time. *Exchange*, 6–10.

Bertacchi, J. (1996). Relationship-based organizations. *Zero to Three, 17*(2) 1, 3–7.

Blase, J., & Blase, J. R. (1994). *Empowering teachers*. Thousand Oaks, CA: Corwin Press.

Block, J. R. (2002). *Seeing double*. New York, NY: Routledge.

Bloom, P. J. (2010). *Measuring work attitudes in the early childhood setting: Technical manual for the Early Childhood Job Satisfaction Survey and the Early Childhood Work Environment Survey*. Wheeling, IL: McCormick Center for Early Childhood Leadership, National-Louis University.

Bloom, P. J. (2005). *Blueprint for Action: Achieving center-based change through staff development*. Lake Forest, IL: New Horizons.

Bloom, P. J. (2000). *Circle of Influence: Implementing shared decision making and participative management*. Lake Forest, IL: New Horizons.

Bolman, L., & Deal, T. (1995). *Leading with soul: An uncommon journey of spirit*. San Francisco, CA: Jossey-Bass.

Bruno, H. E. (2009, November/December). Mary Catherine and me: Building cross-cultural relationships in "post-racial" America. *Exchange*, 26–31.

Buckingham, M. (2007). *Go put your strengths to work*. New York, NY: Free Press.

Carter, M. (2009, November/December). Communities of practice for professional development. *Exchange*, 20–24.

Carter, M. (2004, May/June). Tolerance or transformation: What's our training goal? *Exchange*, 22–24.

Carter, M., & Curtis, D. (2010). *The visionary director: A handbook for dreaming, organizing, and improvising in your center* (2nd ed). St. Paul, MN: Redleaf Press.

Center for the Child Care Workforce. (1998). *Model work standards*. Washington, DC: Author.

Decker, C., Decker, J., Freeman, N., & Knopf, H. (2009). *Planning and administering early childhood programs*. Upper Saddle River, NJ: Merrill.

Denning, S. (2007). *The secret language of leadership: How leaders inspire action through narrative*. San Francisco, CA: Jossey-Bass.

Derman-Sparks, L., & Edwards, J. O. (2010). *Anti-bias education for young children and ourselves*. Washington, DC: NAEYC.

Drucker, P. (2007). *People and performance*. Cambridge, MA: Harvard Business Press.

DuFour, R. (2004, May). What is a "professional learning community"? *Educational Leadership, 61*(8), 6–11.

DuFour, R. (2002, Spring). One clear voice is needed in the din. *Journal of Staff Development, 23*(2), 60–61.

Eisenhauer, M. J., & Pratt, D. (2010, May). Capturing the image of a male preschool teacher. *Young Children, 65*(3), 12–16.

Esty, K., Griffin, R., & Hirsch, M. (1995). *Workplace diversity: A manager's guide to solving problems and turning diversity into a competitive advantage*. Holbrook, MA: Adams Media Corporation.

Fisher, R., & Ury, W. (1991). *Getting to yes: Negotiating agreement without giving in*. New York, NY: Penguin.

Gostick, A., & Elton, C. (2007). *The carrot principle*. New York, NY: Free Press.

Gray, R. (2007). *Climate of success: Creating the right organizational climate for high performance*. Portsmouth, NH: Heinemann.

Greenman, J. T. (2005). Caring spaces, learning places. Redmond, WA: *Exchange* Press.

Greenman, J. (1989, October). Diversity and conflict: The whole world will never sing in perfect harmony. *Exchange*, 11–13.

Guskey, T. (2000). *Evaluating professional development*. Thousand Oaks, CA: Corwin Press.

Hargreaves, A. (1994). *Changing teachers; changing times*. New York, NY: Teachers College Press.

Huseman, R., & Hatfield, J. (1989). *Managing the equity factor*. Boston, MA: Houghton Mifflin.

Kagan, S. L., Kauerz, K., & Tarrant, K. (2008). *The early care and education teaching workforce at the fulcrum: An agenda for reform*. New York, NY: Teachers College Press.

Lightfoot, S. (1983). *Good high schools: Portraits of character and culture*. New York, NY: Basic Books.

Little, J. W. (1982). Norms of collegiality and experimentation: Workplace conditions of school success. *American Educational Research Journal 19*, 325–40.

Lower, J. K., & Cassidy, D. J. (2007, Winter). Child care work environments: The relationship with learning environments. *Journal of Research in Childhood Education, 22*(2), 189–204.

McCormick Center for Early Childhood Leadership. (2010, Spring). A window on early childhood administrative practices. *Research Notes*. Wheeling, IL: National-Louis University.

McGraw, P. (1999). *Life strategies: Doing what works, doing what matters*. New York, NY: Hyperion.

Maurer, R. (2004). *One small step can change your life: The Kaizen way*. New York, NY: Workman.

Michalko, M. (2006). *Thinkertoys: A handbook of creative-thinking techniques*. Berkeley, CA: Ten Speed Press.

National Association for the Education of Young Children. (2010). *A conceptual framework for early childhood professional development: A position statement*. Washington, DC: Author.

National Association for the Education of Young Children and National Association of Early Childhood Specialists in State Departments of Education. (2002). Early learning standards: Creating the conditions for success. *Joint position statement*. http://208.118.177.216/about/positions/pdf/position_statement.pdf.

Palmer, J. (1989) Three paradigms for diversity change leaders. *Organizational Development Practitioner,* 15–18.

Pelo, A. (2006, November/December). Growing a culture of inquiry: Observation as professional development. *Exchange,* 50–53.

Pink, D. (2009). *Drive: The surprising truth about what motivates us.* New York, NY: Riverhead Books.

Reeves, D. B. (2010). *Transforming professional development into student results.* Alexandria, VA: Association for Supervision and Curriculum Development.

Rogers, E. M. (2003) *Diffusion of innovations.* New York, NY: Free Press.

Sciarra, D. J., & Dorsey, A. G. (2009). *Developing and administering a child care and education program* (7th ed.). Clifton Park, NY: Thompson Delmar.

Stringer, R. (2002). *Leadership and organizational climate.* Upper Saddle River, NJ: Prentice Hall.

Talan, T. N., & Bloom, P. J. (2004). *Program Administration Scale: Measuring early childhood leadership and management.* New York, NY: Teachers College Press.

Topsfield Foundation & Reaven, M. (1997). *The busy citizen's discussion guide toward a more perfect union in an age of diversity.* Pomfret, CT: Study Circles Resource Center.

Whitebook, M., & Sakai, L. (2003). Turnover begets turnover: An examination of job and occupational stability among child care center staff. *Early Childhood Research Quarterly, 18*(3), 273–93.

Zmuda, A., Kuklis, R., & Kline, E. (2004). *Transforming schools.* Alexandria, VA: Association for Supervision and Curriculum Development.

Appendices

A.   Early Childhood Work Environment Survey—Short Version

B.   Early Childhood Work Environment Survey

C.   "I Value a Co-Worker Who Is ..."

D.   Role Perceptions Questionnaire

Early Childhood Work Environment Survey
Short Version

This survey is designed to find out how you feel about this early childhood center as a place to work. The success of the survey depends on your candid and honest responses. Please know that your answers are completely confidential; you do not need to sign the form. When you have completed the questionnaire, put it in the attached plain envelope, seal it, and give it to your staff representative.

Indicate in the space provided the numeral (0–5) that most accurately describes how you feel about each statement.

Never 0	Seldom 1	Sometimes 2	Somewhat regularly 3	Frequently 4	Always 5

_____ Staff are friendly and trust one another.

_____ Morale is high. There is a good team spirit.

_____ Staff are encouraged to learn new skills and competencies.

_____ The center provides guidance for professional advancement.

_____ Supervisor(s) are knowledgeable and competent.

_____ Supervisor(s) provide helpful feedback.

_____ Communication regarding policies and procedures is clear.

_____ Job responsibilities are well defined.

_____ Salaries and benefits are distributed equitably.

_____ Promotions are handled fairly.

_____ Teachers help make decisions about things that directly affect them.

_____ People feel free to express their opinions.

_____ Staff agree on school philosophy and educational objectives.

_____ Staff share a common vision of what the center should be like.

_____ The program is well planned and efficiently run.

_____ Meetings are productive. Time is not wasted.

_____ The work environment is attractive and well organized.

_____ There are sufficient supplies and equipment for staff to do their jobs.

_____ Staff are encouraged to be creative and innovative in their work.

_____ The center implements changes as needed.

What three words describe the climate of this center as a place to work?

What do you perceive to be the center's greatest strengths?

What areas do you feel could use some improvement?

Thank you!

McCORMICK CENTER FOR EARLY CHILDHOOD LEADERSHIP
6310 Capitol Drive, Wheeling, Illinois 60090
(800) 443-5522, ext. 5055
http://cecl.nl.edu

Early Childhood Work Environment Survey

Dear Early Childhood Professional:

This survey is designed to find out how you and your colleagues feel about your early childhood center as a place to work. The questionnaire provides you with an opportunity to express your feelings and opinions concerning various center policies and practices. It includes questions about general work conditions, staff relations, supervisor support, pay and promotion opportunities, and the physical setting. The questionnaire should take about 20 minutes to complete. The success of this survey depends on your candid and honest responses. An individual's responses to the survey will not be identified. Results will be reported as group averages that assure anonymity.

When you have completed the survey, put it in the attached plain envelope, seal it, and give it to your staff representative. This individual will then mail the sealed surveys to the McCormick Center for Early Childhood Leadership for data analysis. In approximately six weeks your center will receive a center profile. The profile will report a summary of the group results along ten dimensions. From this profile, staff will be able to systematically determine group perceptions of program strengths as well as identify areas that may need improving.

Thank you for your cooperation and assistance. I hope you find this survey both interesting and useful.

Cordially,

Paula Jorde Bloom

Paula Jorde Bloom, Ph.D.
Chair

Background Information

Sex: ☐ Male ☐ Female   Age: _____ Years

What is the highest educational level you have completed?

☐ High School or GED equivalent   ☐ Some graduate work
☐ Some college   ☐ Master's Degree (MA/MS)
☐ Associate's Degree (AA)   ☐ Post Master's work
☐ Bachelor's Degree (BA/BS)   ☐ Doctorate (Ed.D/Ph.D.)

How long have you worked in
the field of early childhood?   _____ Years _____ Months

How long have you worked for
your current employer?   _____ Years _____ Months

How long have you worked
in your current position?   _____ Years _____ Months

Indicate the category that most nearly describes your present employment:

☐ employed full-time (more than 35 hours per week)
☐ employed part-time (10 to 34 hours per week)

How many months of the year do you work?

☐ 11 or 12 months
☐ 9 or 10 months
☐ fewer than 9 months

Check the job title that most nearly describes your role in your organization. If you have a dual role, what position do you spend *more* time doing?

☐ assistant teacher, aide, or apprentice
☐ teacher
☐ lead teacher
☐ assistant director
☐ director
☐ component coordinator (education, family support, health/nutrition)
☐ support staff (secretary, cook)

Work Attitudes

Check **all** that describe how you feel about your organization:

- ☐ I intend to work here at least two more years
- ☐ I often think of quitting
- ☐ I'm just putting in time
- ☐ I take pride in my center
- ☐ I put a lot of extra effort into my work
- ☐ I feel very committed to this center
- ☐ I don't care what happens to this place after I leave
- ☐ It would be difficult for me to find another job as good as this one
- ☐ It's hard to feel committed to this place
- ☐ I sometimes feel trapped in this job

If you could design the ideal job, how close would your present position resemble this ideal position with respect to the following? *(check 1–5)*

	not like my ideal at all	somewhat like my ideal			is my ideal
	1	2	3	4	5
relationship with your co-workers	☐	☐	☐	☐	☐
opportunities to learn and grow	☐	☐	☐	☐	☐
relationship with your supervisor	☐	☐	☐	☐	☐
clarity in roles and responsibilities	☐	☐	☐	☐	☐
fairness of pay and promotion opportunities	☐	☐	☐	☐	☐
decision-making structure of the center	☐	☐	☐	☐	☐
agreement among staff on program goals	☐	☐	☐	☐	☐
task orientation, program efficiency	☐	☐	☐	☐	☐
equipment, materials, and the physical setting	☐	☐	☐	☐	☐
innovativeness and creative problem solving	☐	☐	☐	☐	☐

Different people want and expect different things from their work. Check the **3** aspects of your work that are most important to you:

- ☐ collegiality, co-worker relations
- ☐ opportunities for professional growth
- ☐ support and feedback from supervisor
- ☐ clarity in policies and procedures
- ☐ fairness in pay, benefits, and promotions
- ☐ involvement in decision making
- ☐ consensus on program goals and objectives
- ☐ accomplishing work in an efficient manner
- ☐ physical setting, sufficient materials
- ☐ innovativeness and creative expression

Organizational Climate

Please answer the questions in this section with respect to the overall conditions in your center as they are *most of the time*:

Check *all* that describe the staff relations in your center most of the time:

- ☐ cooperative and friendly
- ☐ competitive
- ☐ people are reluctant to express their feelings
- ☐ teachers are very helpful to new staff
- ☐ good team spirit
- ☐ staff are generally frank and candid
- ☐ morale is low
- ☐ people socialize outside of work
- ☐ people feel isolated
- ☐ people complain a lot

Check *all* that apply. Does your center...

- ☐ provide on-site staff development workshops?
- ☐ encourage staff to share resources with one another?
- ☐ provide release time to attend conferences?
- ☐ provide release time to visit other schools?
- ☐ provide tuition reimbursement to take college courses?
- ☐ provide guidance for professional advancement?
- ☐ have a library of professional books for staff to use?
- ☐ subscribe to several educational journals and magazines?
- ☐ implement a career ladder for professional advancement?
- ☐ encourage staff to learn new skills and competencies?

Check *all* that characterize the supervision provided at your center most of the time:

- ☐ provides support and helpful feedback
- ☐ hard to please
- ☐ unavailable
- ☐ conducts fair evaluations of staff
- ☐ too critical
- ☐ sets high but realistic standards
- ☐ delegates too much
- ☐ compliments and praises staff
- ☐ talks down to staff
- ☐ very knowledgeable

Check *all* that apply. Does your program...

- ☐ distribute a parent handbook detailing policies and procedures?
- ☐ have a staff manual outlining staff policies?
- ☐ provide written contracts for employees?
- ☐ have written job descriptions for each position?
- ☐ distribute a monthly newsletter to parents?

Check *all* that characterize your center most of the time:

- ☐ written communication is clear
- ☐ there are seldom conflicting demands made on staff
- ☐ policies and procedures are well-defined
- ☐ rules are consistent
- ☐ staff are well-informed

Check *all* that describe the pay and promotion system at your center:

- ☐ salaries are fair considering the center's income
- ☐ promotions are not handled fairly
- ☐ pay and benefits are equitably distributed
- ☐ some people are paid more than they are worth
- ☐ raises are based on favoritism
- ☐ steps are being taken to increase pay and benefits
- ☐ pay is fair compared to what other centers pay
- ☐ this place is a revolving door, no job security
- ☐ people are taken advantage of
- ☐ chances for promotion are good

Check *all* that describe how decisions are made at your center most of the time:

- ☐ people are encouraged to be self-sufficient in making decisions
- ☐ the director likes to make most of the decisions
- ☐ people don't feel free to express their opinions
- ☐ everyone provides input on the content of staff meetings
- ☐ conformity is the name of the game here
- ☐ there are scheduled staff meetings at least twice a month
- ☐ people provide input but decisions have already been made
- ☐ teachers make decisions about things that directly affect them
- ☐ teachers are seldom asked their opinion on issues
- ☐ the director values everyone's input for major decisions

Listed below are some common organizational decisions and actions. How much influence does the teaching staff *currently have* in each of the areas below:

	very little influence	some influence	considerable influence
Ordering materials/supplies	☐	☐	☐
Interviewing/hiring new staff	☐	☐	☐
Determining program objectives	☐	☐	☐
Training new aides/teachers	☐	☐	☐
Planning daily schedule of activities	☐	☐	☐

How much influence do you think the teaching staff *would like to have* in each of these areas:

	very little influence	some influence	considerable influence
Ordering materials/supplies	☐	☐	☐
Interviewing/hiring new staff	☐	☐	☐
Determining program objectives	☐	☐	☐
Training new aides/teachers	☐	☐	☐
Planning daily schedule of activities	☐	☐	☐

Check *all* that apply with respect to the goals of your program:

- ☐ goals are left vague
- ☐ everyone agrees on program goals
- ☐ people know how to compromise
- ☐ center does not have a written philosophy
- ☐ staff share a common vision of what the center should be like
- ☐ staff seldom talk about educational objectives
- ☐ staff are committed to program goals
- ☐ staff are not unified in their philosophy
- ☐ people disagree on what should be taught to children
- ☐ program has well-defined educational objectives

Check *all* that describe the way things get done at your center most of the time:

- ☐ meetings are a waste of time
- ☐ this place is run very efficiently
- ☐ there is a focus on results and program outcomes
- ☐ time is wasted; there are lost opportunities
- ☐ deadlines are missed regularly
- ☐ people are held accountable
- ☐ employees work hard
- ☐ people come to work late
- ☐ people procrastinate often
- ☐ meetings are productive

Check *all* that apply to the physical environment of your center:

- ☐ efficient use of space
- ☐ cramped and crowded conditions
- ☐ seems either too hot or too cold
- ☐ neat, tidy, and safe
- ☐ decorations are drab
- ☐ teachers have a place to store personal belongings
- ☐ classroom noise disrupts office business
- ☐ there are sufficient supplies and materials
- ☐ the building needs major repairs
- ☐ storage space is well-organized

Check *all* that describe your program as a whole:

- ☐ emphasizes creativity
- ☐ not very innovative
- ☐ quite traditional
- ☐ implements needed changes
- ☐ encourages diverse opinions
- ☐ regularly looks at new educational approaches
- ☐ things stay pretty much the same
- ☐ new ideas are tried out
- ☐ people avoid taking risks at all costs
- ☐ problems are not addressed

Rank order the following program objectives according to their importance at your center during the next year. Put a "1" by the most important, a "2" by the next most important and so on until you get to "6" for the least important. Each objective must have only *one* number next to it.

In our program, it is important...

_____ to help children develop language and problem-solving skills

_____ to help children build strong friendships and learn to share

_____ to help children master concepts needed for reading and arithmetic

_____ to help children develop skill and independence in caring for themselves

_____ to help children develop physical coordination

_____ to help children develop healthy self-esteem and a positive self-concept

How long did it take you to complete this survey? _____ minutes

We appreciate your cooperation in taking the time to answer the questions in this survey. If you have any additional comments you would like to add, feel free to do so in the space below. Again, thank you.

I value a co-worker who is . . .

☐ Ambitious (hard working, aspiring)

☐ Broadminded (open to new ideas and feedback)

☐ Capable (competent, effective)

☐ Clean (neat, tidy)

☐ Cheerful (lighthearted, joyful)

☐ Collaborative (contributes to group efforts)

☐ Compassionate (shows empathy)

☐ Courageous (stands up for beliefs)

☐ Forgiving (willing to pardon others)

☐ Fun (good sense of humor)

☐ Helpful (concerned about the welfare of others)

☐ Honest (sincere, truthful)

☐ Imaginative (creative)

☐ Independent (self-reliant, self-sufficient)

☐ Intelligent (smart, reflective)

☐ Logical (consistent, rational)

☐ Loving (affectionate, caring)

☐ Obedient (follows policies and procedures)

☐ Polite (courteous, well-mannered)

☐ Respectful (shows positive regard for others)

☐ Responsible (dependable, reliable)

☐ Self-Controlled (restrained, self-disciplined)

Bloom, P. J., Hentschel, A., & Bella, J. (2010) *A Great Place to Work*. Lake Forest, IL: New Horizons. (www.newhorizonsbooks.net)

Role Perceptions Questionnaire

For each of the 12 items, please circle the response that most accurately describes your feelings about your job.

	Seldom		Sometimes		Always
1. I am clear about what my responsibilities are.	1	2	3	4	5
2. I am certain about how much authority I have.	1	2	3	4	5
3. I am given a chance to do the things I do best.	1	2	3	4	5
4. I have an opportunity to develop my own special abilities.	1	2	3	4	5
5. I spend time on unnecessary, irrelevant tasks.	1	2	3	4	5
6. Clear planned goals and objectives exist for my job.	1	2	3	4	5
7. I receive conflicting expectations from people about my job.	1	2	3	4	5
8. I have the knowledge and skills to do my job well.	1	2	3	4	5
9. I have enough resources to do my job well.	1	2	3	4	5
10. There is enough time to do my job well.	1	2	3	4	5
11. I ignore certain policies in order to carry out my job.	1	2	3	4	5
12. I get the support I need to do my job well.	1	2	3	4	5

What keeps you from being as effective as you would like to be in your position?

If you had the power to change anything about your job, what would you change? Why would this be an improvement over existing conditions?

What suggestions do you have for improving schedules, routines, and procedures so staff can function as a more effective team?

Scoring

Add up the numerals circled for all items except 5, 7, and 11. Because these three items are worded negatively, reverse the scoring (seldom = 5, always = 1) and add them to the total. A respondent's total score on this questionnaire will range from 12 to 60. A high score (48–60) indicates that staff perceive that their jobs are clearly defined and they seldom experience conflicting demands and role expectations. A low average score (12–24) indicates that confusion exists about lines of authority and role assignments.

From Bloom, P. J. (2005). *Blueprint for action: Achieving center-based change through staff development* (pp. 268–269). Lake Forest, IL: New Horizons. Reprinted with permission.

Available from New Horizons

- Avoiding Burnout: Managing Time, Space, and People in Early Childhood Education

- Blueprint for Action: Achieving Center-Based Change Through Staff Development

- Workshop Essentials: Planning and Presenting Dynamic Workshops

- The Program Administration Scale: Measuring Early Childhood Leadership and Management

- The Business Administration Scale for Family Child Care

The Director's Toolbox:
A Management Series for Early Childhood Administrators

- Circle of Influence: Implementing Shared Decision Making and Participative Management

- Making the Most of Meetings: A Practical Guide

- The Right Fit: Recruiting, Selecting, and Orienting Staff

- Leadership in Action: How Effective Directors Get Things Done

- From the Inside Out: The Power of Reflection and Self-Awareness

A Trainer's Guide is also available for each topic in the Director's Toolbox Series. Each guide provides step-by-step instructions for planning and presenting a dynamic and informative six-hour workshop. Included are trainers' notes and presentation tips, instructions for conducting learning activities, reproducible handouts, transparencies, and a PowerPoint CD presentation.

To place your order or receive additional information
on prices and quantity discounts, contact:

NEW HORIZONS
P.O. Box 863
Lake Forest, Illinois 60045-0863
(847) 295-8131
(815) 366-7494 FAX
newhorizons4@comcast.net
www.newhorizonsbooks.net